PLAYING GOD?

ENGINEERING WITH GENES

PLAYING GOD?

ENGINEERING WITH GENES

BY JOHN NEWELL
ILLUSTRATIONS BY HILARY PAYNTER

© Copyright John Newell 1991

First published in 1991
by Broadside Books Limited
2 Gurney Road,
London E15 1SH

ISBN 0-9515629-5-9

Design:
The Studio
15 Soho Square,
London W1

Typesetting:
Bow Towning Limited
33-41 Dallington Street,
London EC1V 0BB

Printed by:
Bookbuilders
Hong Kong

CONTENTS

Introduction		9
Chapter 1	What is Genetic Engineering?	13
Chapter 2	The Genetic Engineer's Photocopier	19
Chapter 3	Gene Therapy	22
Chapter 4	Diagnosing Defects	31
Chapter 5	Superdrugs for the 21st Century	41
Chapter 6	Antibodies: Immunity's Guided Missiles	48
Chapter 7	New Vaccines for Old Diseases	56
Chapter 8	Cancer and Oncogenes	68
Chapter 9	The Handbook of Man	71
Chapter 10	Biotransformations: Enzymes and Antibodies in Industry	75
Chapter 11	Transgenic Animals	83
Chapter 12	Transgenic Plants	92
Chapter 13	Abraham Lincoln and the First Americans	103
Postscript		106
Index		109

INTRODUCTION

In the spring of 1989 I stood holding out a hopeful microphone to passers-by hurrying down the hill of Surrey Street from offices around Bush House, headquarters of the World Service, to the Temple underground station on the Embankment. They were on their way to catch their trains home and I was "doing a vox pop" – asking them to tell me what they thought about genetic engineering – for two radio programmes called "Playing God?".

I had thought the title was provocative, a little too inclined to assume that people must have doubts about the whole idea of genetic engineering. But it soon became clear that, so far as the men and women in the street were concerned, playing God (without any question mark), usurping powers that ought to belong to Him alone (even if they weren't sure there was a Him), is what genetic engineers are seen to be doing. That was the uncontested view of old, of young, of male, of female, of educated and of uneducated alike. "And", said the voice of the people, "genetic engineers should stop, now, before God, or Nature takes his or its terrible revenge".

Later, answering questions about genetic engineering on radio "phone-ins", I met the same attitude. The very idea filled the audience with foreboding. Genetic engineering was something tremendous, something fearful, something awesome. But quite what was this awesome, tremendous something, nobody seemed quite sure.

AWESOME POWERS

As is usually the case, the instinct of the public is, in one way, absolutely right. The powers conferred on Man by genetic engineering are of a different order to those conferred by anything else except, perhaps, the hydrogen bomb. But while that power is wholly destructive, the power of genetic engineering may be used for a huge variety of purposes – the great majority of which can make us and our fellow creatures healthier, happier, better fed and better off. It is also true that genetic engineering may be misused; to widen the gap between an affluent, powerful North and an impoverished, dependent South, to increase rather than diminish the sufferings of humans and of animals, conceivably to produce deadlier weapons of germ warfare.

We should not be misled by the apparently

cautious claims of the scientists themselves. Scientists, writing or talking about their work, are concerned not to appear big-headed, not to make fools of themselves in the eyes of their fellow scientists. They tend to play down the importance of their research, and utter endless cautions about how it may not work and how they still have far to go. But once you learn their language and discover just how far they have already gone in the first ten years of genetic engineering, when you see the procedures that are now routine in the laboratory, you realise that in reality genetic engineering is moving at hurricane pace.

SENSATIONALISM

Every science has its own language which has to be interpreted before a writer can start to say something about it. Every science writer should be an interpreter as well as a reporter. Scientists often accuse journalists distorting the picture by writing far too much about problems and dangers and not nearly enough about promise and potential. When we do write about their achievements, say scientists, we distort them by being too premature, describing discoveries that will take several years (and may never happen at all) as if they were immediately imminent.

There is much truth in both allegations. And as well as bad journalism, there is the great self-righteous scaremongering industry that works tirelessly and irresponsibly to feed on the public's natural caution and awe, turning that right and sensible feeling into something approaching paranoia.

EFFECT ON CAREERS

The bad image genetic engineering has acquired is frightening bright young people away from the study of biotechnology and genetic engineering just when they should be encouraged to choose it as a career precisely because it is going to be so important. The kind of people who ought to be in charge of the awesome developments coming in twenty years time aren't being trained now – or at least, not enough of them are. Too many of the best brains go to work in financial services paying higher salaries and offering more security than can be obtained in pure or applied science.

Nor are there enough of the young idealists with fire in their bellies who will be needed to drive biotechnology where it ought to go. Too many of them are still turning to the social sciences where they will have far less chance to change the world for the good.

In the end the future of biotechnology depends on it producing things people want to buy, whether such products are bought by you and I over the counter or by people in industry to use in factories. If the image of things made by genetic engineering is a bad image, then people won't buy them. Then big companies will shy away from the use of biotechnology because they can't afford to take that risk, not with their competitors proclaiming in advertisements that "No Genetically Engineered Organism is Used in the Preparation of This Product".

If people don't buy and industry doesn't make products using genetic engineering, then not only will there be fewer and fewer jobs for genetic engineers in industry. There will also be fewer and fewer jobs in universities, for in the end there are very severe limits on the numbers of staff universities can afford to keep working on subjects of no practical importance.

The cycle goes like this: new technology throws up new possibilities which journalists tell the public about. The public decides whether it loves or hates them and what it wants done with them. And in the end the government follows the public's lead. With genetic engineering this cycle has been broken because the public has not been told. The public knows something colossal is happening, but it doesn't understand it. Sensibly, it is cautious and even afraid. There is a great need to inform the public properly so as to rejoin the broken cycle and enable the public to take control and use its voice again.

A SCIENTIST'S VIEWPOINT

I find that most of the scientists involved feel the full weight of their responsibilities to the public. One leading researcher (involved in making antibodies, the body's natural defences against disease), Dr. Greg Winter of the Cambridge Laboratory for Molecular Biology, put it like this:

"I think it's up to us, as we are the first people to make discoveries and perhaps the first to see implications, and the first to have all the information at our fingertips. We have the responsibility to draw attention to it. But the problem is that we don't want to trigger a witch-hunt by drawing attention to it. I think one of the problems we face is to try to draw attention to problems but only in a quiet and responsible manner."

It is little exaggeration to say that, in today's climate, genetic engineers cannot win. If they publicise their work it is liable to be distorted into blood-curdling headlines. If they refuse to publicise, they give cause for all those doubts which have their base in fear of the unknown and distrust of secrecy. In order to resolve this dilemma, not only must scientists be prepared to work at communicating, but journalists must be responsible in handling their material.

Public "Abysmally Prepared?"

If all this is the case, can we hope that the public will pick up the reins and tell the government exactly what it does and does not want done with genetic engineering? Professor Theodore Friedmann of the University of California at San Diego who has been involved in discussing the ethics of and drawing up regulations for genetic engineering, gave me a largely negative answer to this question:

"I think our publics are abysmally prepared for the knowledge that's coming in the modern world. We really need to undertake a much more effective programmes for getting information to the public, with TV programmes and discussion and much better programmes of education in our schools. I think we need an informed, educated public in science as in all other realms, and I don't have any doubts that an informed public will be a public that can use this kind of knowledge well. An uniformed public can be manipulated by demagogues and by people with motives that are not always in the public interest. An unenlightened public that can be led around like that is a dangerous public and the solution to that is enlightenment and information and education."

I hope this book will contribute something towards that end. Its aim is to help you to understand the colossal powers of genetic engineering so that, having understood, you won't want to put it all back in the box and close the lid. You will know instead how to use the enormous power of public pressure to make your government, and the industries whose products you buy or use, employ those powers in ways you want and of which you wholeheartedly approve.

The Modern Promotheus?

Will today's geneticist live to regret tampering with the secrets of Life?

CHAPTER 1

WHAT IS GENETIC ENGINEERING?

So what is genetic engineering? What's it all about? The term is a bit misleading because it implies improving on genes – engineering them. That is only just starting to be done. What is being done now, and has been developing over the last ten to fifteen years (depending on what area of genetic engineering we are looking at) is the business of moving genes from one living organism to another. This ability to move genes around is being used in several different ways, and for different purposes – some much more advanced than others. We will look at them all first, very briefly here, and then in greater detail later in the book.

So far, the most advanced and widely used way of moving genes around is that which involves moving genes into cultures of living cells grown in laboratories. The main aim of this is to make some of the substances that control the human body's internal chemistry – especially our defences against disease – outside (ital) the body in large quantities, so that they can be used in exactly the same way as medical drugs.

A second activity which is just beginning, but which will certainly receive more publicity than all other types of genetic engineering put together, is what is called gene therapy. This involves the treatment of people affected by incurable diseases which are caused by defective genes, that wait like little time-bombs in their DNA, or genetic make-up. The treatment involves putting the correct version of the defective gene into that part of the body affected by disease as a prevention or cure for the disease.

A third type of genetic engineering involves moving genes into plants. This is already being done, and is much further advanced than human gene therapy. Not surprisingly, the aim here is to produce improved and disease-resistant crops more quickly and efficiently than can be done by present plant-breeding methods. Moving genes from one species to another will open up the whole plant and even animal world to breeders searching for improved performance.

Watson and Crick, the Cambridge discoverers of DNA.

Finally, genes are being added to animals: either laboratory animals for research purposes, or to improve the milk yield, body weight, lean to fat ratio and disease resistance of farm animals. A final, ambitious reason for adding genes to animals is so as to use their bodies harmlessly to produce new medical drugs based on the human body's own natural defences, thus dispensing with laborious and time-consuming cell cultures grown in the laboratory.

WHAT IS A GENE?

A gene is a blueprint for making a single protein in that bit of the body which contains the gene. A human body, yours or mine, contains roughly one hundred thousand genes. Most of them are exactly the same in every human being.

Proteins are chemicals, but they are not the sort of chemicals that non-chemists, or even chemists who are not biochemists, are familiar with. A typical protein molecule contains several thousand atoms. It is made up of a long chain of sub-units called amino acids. Although each protein molecule is a single long chain, the chain is curled up like a ball of string of a very precise three-dimensional shape, different for each protein. The shapes of protein molecules are what life is all about.

The shape of any one protein is exactly suited to its particular job. It may be an antibody – one of the protein molecules which fastens onto and helps to destroy enemy micro- organisms (bacteria or viruses) which get into our bodies. Another differently shaped protein molecule may be an enzyme – one of the natural catalysts, each of which catalyses one of the several thousand complex chemical reactions going on inside us.

Each of the hundred thousand different proteins in our body has a different function. Only proteins are molecules large enough to perform complex bodily functions, like catalysing reactions or neutralising viruses. The other chemicals in our bodies perform simple functions, acting as stores of fuel or as strengthening materials, for example. Our genes determine the exact structures of the proteins which make us human, because we have most of them in common with all other humans. We have many of them in common with animals as well. And genes are also responsible for that tiny proportion of proteins which makes you different to me.

HOW GENES ARE INHERITED

This is where heredity comes in. Half of our genes, as we have learnt at school, come from our mother, and half from our father. In fact, that isn't quite true. There are some genes that we inherit only through our mothers, and these are called

A Mitochondrion.

mitochondrial genes. They are found in the tiny structures called mitochondria inside living cells. The reason we can only inherit these genes through our mothers is because eggs contain mitochondria, but sperms are so small that they have no room for them.

These mitochondrial genes are more than just a curiosity. Because they are inherited only through the female line, scientists have claimed that they have used them to trace the ancestry of the human race back to a single woman living in Africa 200,000 years ago – a real-life Eve.

INHERITED DEFECTS

If there is a defect in the gene of one of our parents, we may, if we are unlucky, inherit the defect and the disease it causes. One the other hand, we may escape. This is because there are two copies of every gene in every cell of the body. The human body contains thousands of millions of

African Eve: our common ancestor.

cells: bone cells, brain cells, blood cells, skin cells and so on. Each cell contains a double set of all the 100,000 genes that, between them, are the complete blueprints needed for making that body. Every gene in every cell, except in the reproductive cells, is duplicated.

The reproductive cells, sperms and eggs, have only one copy of each gene. This is so that when the sperm fertilizes the egg, the resulting fertilized egg will once more have two of every gene, one contributed by the mother and one by the father. All the cells in the body that grow from that egg will go on to have one of each pair of genes derived from each parent.

When sperms and eggs are formed by other cells dividing, the process is called reduction divison. Instead of the cells formed by reduction division having two of each gene, as happens after every other kind of cell division, the reproductive cells have only one of each gene. When a cell divides to form a sperm or an egg, one of each of the cell's pairs of genes goes into the new sperm or egg. The other member of the pair goes into the other product of the divison: a functionless cell called a polar body.

This explains the Russian Roulette of why defective genes are sometimes inherited, and sometimes not. If only one of a pair of genes is defective, then there is a fifty-fifty chance that it will get into the egg or sperm and so on into the child that grows from them. There is an equal chance that the defective gene will end up after reduction division in the functionless polar body.

This is not just a useless piece of scientific information. It is the basis of a very new technique which is now beginning to be used for diagnosing genetic defects by examining unfertilized eggs, rather than embryos. This is making it possible to prevent not only the birth but even the conception of foetuses affected by some genetic defects. It is much more acceptable to religious and other groups opposed to searches for genetic defects on foetuses which expose them to the possibility of being aborted if defects are discovered.

Each cell in the body, apart from the reproductive cells, contains two complete, identical sets of around 100,000 genes. How is it that these sets of instructions which are identical, be they in a bone cell or a brain cell, produce such different cells with such very different functions?

How Cells Differentiate

The answer is that only some of the genes in each cell are 'switched on', so to speak. The rest are not working. In the language of the genetic engineer, only a small proportion of genes in each cell are being expressed. This means the cell is only making the proteins which those genes code for – for which they act as blueprint. The rest of the genes (probably the majority of them) in each cell are suppressed.

In a bone cell, for example, only the small proportion of its one hundred thousand genes which are need to perform all the functions of bone cells are expressed. In a brain cell of the same person, a different (though overlapping) set of genes are expressed. Very few, if any, genes are expressed right through a cell's life. Most genes are expressed for relatively short periods, while the cell has need of a particular gene's product – as the protein made according to the gene's blueprint is called.

The 'switches' – actually biochemical reactions

that turn genes on and off – are of great practical use to biotechnology. Genetic engineers want to be able to manipulate these switches, and have already got hold of some of them. The intention is to use the switches to switch on the expression of genes which have been moved into cell cultures, or to switch them off when required.

A selection of specialised cells.

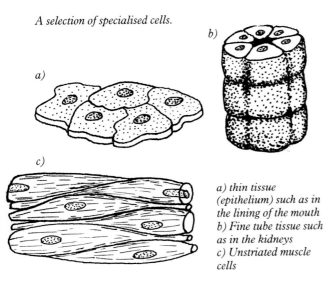

*a) thin tissue (epithelium) such as in the lining of the mouth
b) Fine tube tissue such as in the kidneys
c) Unstriated muscle cells*

BIOREACTORS

Cell cultures are grown in a bioreactor. This is basically a big pot in which cells are grown, and into which they secrete their precious chemical products. Bioreactors can be as high as a two-storey house. A whole new branch of engineering is blossoming around the business of designing and running bioreactors, so as to make them produce their products in a smooth, regular and controlled way.

The most advanced bioreactors are 'intelligent' bioreactors, so-called because the way in which the cells in them are fed with the nutrients they require to live and produce their product, as well as the temperature and the timing of the removal of this product are all computer-controlled.

Switching cells on or off in bioreactors is one use for the switches that control the expression of genes. Another potential use is in medicine. An incurable brain condition, Parkinson's disease, is being treated experimentally by implanting brain cells taken from early aborted foetuses into the brains of those suffering from the disease. At the time of writing, results are just starting to suggest that this procedure may really benefit the patients.

If this is proved, then there will be a colossal (and controversial) demand for foetal brain tissue. And if, as a number of scientists and doctors think may happen, similar treatments could help other commonly occurring conditions, such as Alzheimers disease (a form of pre-senile dementia which afflicts millions of people), then the demand for foetal cells could become uncontrollably vast.

There would be a growing danger that poor women in countries where medical controls are lax would accept offers to become pregnant in order to have abortions to satisfy the demand for precious foetal cells for brain and other tissue transplants. Even if this doesn't happen, many people – and not just those opposed to abortion on principle – are very uneasy about the idea of using such cell tissue for medical purposes.

Genetic engineering may offer an alternative. At present, only brain can be used to repair brain, because only brain cells have the right properties. But just suppose there was a way of transforming other kinds of human cells grown in the laboratory into brain cells. In that case, any cell culture – skin cells, for example – could be used to provide the implants to treat disease, with no objections from anyone.

What is needed is the knowledge of how to turn on the switches that make a cell function like a brain cell. Once scientists have discovered this – which is, in effect, discovering which proteins make which genes express themselves – then they can use those proteins to create brain cells, or any other kind of cells needed for medical treatment – whenever required. The use of foetal tissues will have become unnecessary.

MORE ABOUT GENES

Let us now look in more detail at the genes themselves. Each one of the hundred thousand or so genes in each of the billions of cells in the

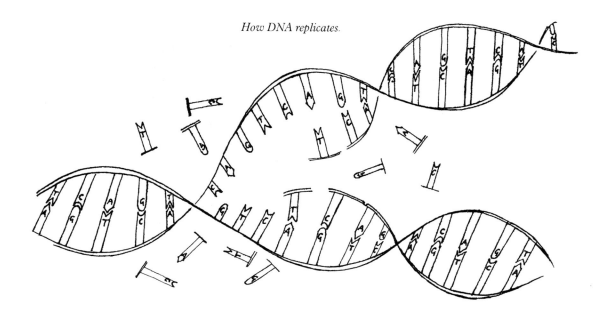

How DNA replicates.

human body codes for one protein, for making one of the working parts of the living cell containing it. The genes are made of DNA: deoxyribonucleic acid, to give it its full name. In 1954 two Cambridge scientists, the American James Watson and the Englishman Francis Crick, discovered how DNA carries the genetic code, and how genes made of DNA are able to be the blueprints for making proteins.

Genes are stored safely in the centres of cells, in a blob called the nucleus, which is surrounded by a membrane. Inside the cell are twenty three pairs of rods called chromosomes. Inside the chromosomes are the very long, thread-like, tightly coiled molecules of DNA. Each DNA molecule is a single long chain made up of sub-units called bases.

THE GENETIC CODES

There are only four different bases: adenine, thymine, guanine and cytosine, known for short as A, T, G and C. Reading along a DNA molecule you might find ATCGTAFCTACGAT, and so on. A DNA molecule is a long, long chain with many thousands of bases as its links in sequence along its length. Each gene is a stretch of DNA usually

between one and two thousand bases in length. Meaningless 'spacer' DNA separates successive genes.

The true secret of life, the genetic code itself, lies in the order in which a thousand or so bases are arranged along the length of each gene. This sequence determines the corresponding sequence of the sub-units of the protein that the gene codes for. These sub-units are amino acids. They form the links along the length of the protein chain.

The first triplet of bases along the gene chain, say ATG, determines which out of twenty amino acids will be the first along the protein chain. Three bases code for one amino acid. The second triplet of bases in the gene determines the second amino acid along the protein, and so on, for as many triplets as it takes to specify the entire protein molecule.

The sequence of amino acids in the protein chain in turn determines the three-dimensional structure of the protein molecule. That shape is what fits the protein molecule for its job – working as an enzyme catalysing a reaction, or as an antibody fastening itself onto a virus, for example. Proteins comprise all the important working and

The sequence of bases in genes.

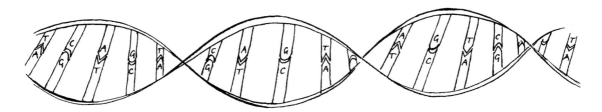

structural parts of all living things, plant and animal. So in this way, the genetic code – the sequence of bases in genes – lays down the structure of every living thing.

The code is the same for all of them: if you take a gene out of any living thing – a man, woman, dog, an apple tree or a mushroom, a fish or a bacterium, and put it into any other living thing, the gene can be made to work in its new home.

BELLS AND WHISTLES!

A gene can't, however, just be snipped out of one cell's DNA and snipped into another. In order to work in its new home, the transplanted gene will need a few bits and pieces tacked onto it. These are the things which genetic engineers refer to frivolously as "Bells and Whistles". The "bells and whistles", which include the switches mentioned earlier and the signals the gene needs to start working in its new environment, may differ from the signals it needed in its old home.

With the right bells and whistles tacked onto it, the gene for a human protein such as insulin, which needs to be injected by diabetics, can be

Bells and whistles...

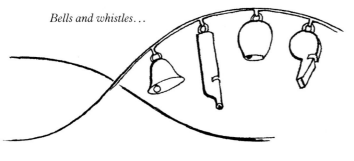

taken out of any human cell, and put into other cells grown as cultures in the laboratory. Then these cells with their added human gene can be put into a bioreactor, where they will grow and divide into really big cultures. All the cells in these cultures have added human genes, which will have been duplicated along with all the cells' other genes each time the cells divide. This multiplication of added genes is known as cloning. In this case, all the cells in the culture will produce insulin, having obeyed the instructions of the added gene (with the right bells and whistles tacked onto it) just as they obey the instructions of their own genes.

INSULIN AND INTERFERON

This is how insulin and interferons – human body substances which combat cancer and some other human diseases – are now being made. Other proteins produced in this way are human growth hormones and, more recently, a number of potent human body control substances known as cytokines or interleukins, which can help to fight diseases in various ways.

We noted earlier that this moving of human genes into cell cultures to make human gene products to use as drugs is the most advanced of the various activities which involve moving genes around. However, human gene therapy – inserting genes not into cell cultures but directly into people to try and cure diseases, is what touches us all most closely. Approval has only recently been given for the first attempts to cure human diseases using gene therapy, and these are now underway. (see chapter 3)

CHAPTER 2

THE GENETIC ENGINEER'S PHOTOCOPIER

When gene cloning was first developed, it seemed an almost miraculous technology. To be able to transfer genes from a cell of any living organism into quite a different kind of cell grown in a laboratory culture, and to watch the added genes multiply along with the cells' own genes, was remarkable indeed. But the speed with which genes can be multiplied in this way isn't fast enough for today's medical research and diagnosis and forensic detective work, all of which need genes to be copied millions of times over. In the case of forensic evidence, for example, enough genes are needed to indicate reliably and quickly from blood or sperm stains which suspect may have committed a murder or a rape. In diagnosing diseases such as cancer, the researcher needs to decide from a few cells from deep in a person's body not only whether the patient has cancer, but what sort and requiring what kind of treatment. Diagnosing the genetic defects which carry disease can now be done in the early foetus, and for this enough genes need to be multiplied quickly from a tiny sample of foetal tissue.

PCR = THE "PHOTOCOPIER"

For such purposes the Polymerase Chain Reaction was devised. Known for short as PCR, it's the geneticist's answer to the photocopier. To understand how it works we need to understand more about DNA.

We've seen that genes are made of DNA, and that the long molecules of DNA, along which are dotted the meaningful sequences which are our genes, are stored in the rods called chromosomes in the nuclei of our cells. The molecules of DNA form a double spiral, the famous double helix, and there is a very important reason for this double spiral: the ability to replicate.

There are just four different kinds of sub-unit out of which DNA molecules are made, four different bases, adenine, thymine, guanine and cytosine, known as A, T, G and C for short. Each successive triplet of bases along the length of a gene determines one amino acid along the corresponding chain of the protein molecule made according to the instructions of the gene.

Imagine one of the two spiral strands of a DNA double helix on its own. Along its length are the bases, in their meaningful sequence. The other spiral molecule of the double spiral is of course also made up of bases. Its bases are joined to the bases of the first molecule by chemical forces, not powerful forces but strong enough to hold the two spirals intertwined together.

The bases in the second spiral are not in the same sequence as those in the first spiral. They are in a complementary sequence, determined by the fact that each base in one spiral pairs off naturally with another base in the other. Adenine pairs with thymine and guanine with cytosine. If you think of the bases joined to each other in the double spiral as rungs in a spiral ladder, then each rung is made of either an adenine-thymine or a cytosine-guanine pair.

It is this pairing off of bases that makes DNA self-replicating. When a cell divides and new sets of genes for the new cells are needed, each double helix of DNA splits into its two separate strands. Then a new complementary strand is built up opposite each single strand. Two double spirals are formed, each identical to the original double spiral.

The assembling of new strands is performed by an enzyme called DNA Polymerase because it polymerases DNA. That's to say it makes polymers, long-chain molecules which are new strands of DNA. It does this by arranging lots of little molecules, or bases, opposite their opposite numbers (the bases they pair with) on an existing strand of DNA. Then the polymerase joins all the bases together into a new strand of DNA twined round the first one.

When a gene sends its instructions out into the cell for a new protein molecule to be made, according to the instructions of the gene, something similar but a bit different happens. The two strands of the section of DNA containing the gene separate and a complementary spiral is assembled along the meaningful strand. But this time it isn't made along the whole length of all the DNA and all the genes in the cell, as would be necessary if a new cell were being made, but only along the length of the gene which is to be expressed.

This new strand is made of a substance slightly different from DNA, known as RNA (ribonucleic acid). When the strand of RNA complementary to the gene is complete, it is detached and sent out of the nucleus into the cell to a ribosome, one of the

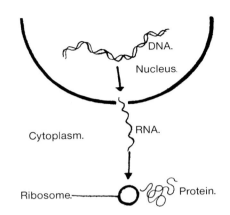

DNA making a complementary strand of RNA to make a new protein.

organelles where new proteins are made. At the ribosome, little bits of RNA become attached to the messenger RNA molecule. Each is a triplet of bases complementary to the triplet it becomes attached to.

In this way the triplets reconstitute the original, meaningful sequence of DNA in the gene. Each triplet carries attached to it a single amino acid. As the amino acids join together they build up a new protein molecule according to the original instructions of the gene.

TELLING PCR WHAT TO COPY

PCR, the Polymerase Chain Reaction, uses the DNA polymerase, that assembles new complementary strands of DNA, to copy genes for any required purpose. PCR was first put to work by Dr. Kary Mullis of the Cetus Corporation. He suddenly realised one day that DNA polymerase could be set to work without the natural controls that it has inside cells. It could be made to start working on any chosen double spiral of DNA which had been made to separate into its two strands artificially. This could easily be done by gently warming up the DNA. Then the polymerase would make two double spirals. If they were again gently heated they would separate again and make four. If they in turn were gently heated, the polymerase would make eight. Then sixteen. Then thirty-two. Then sixty-four. Then 128 and so on. Only twenty such cycles, each taking only a minute or so, would produce more than a million copies of one original double spiral of DNA.

BELLS AND WHISTLES AGAIN

PCR is now used routinely in this way to make millions of copies of any gene of interest which, for one reason or another, is present in very small quantities. DNA polymerase can be instructed to make copies of any required gene by providing the the polymerase with the appropriate 'bell' or 'whistle'. This is a primer, a short sequence of DNA which tells the polymerase where to start making the new complementary strand of DNA.

When the sample to be copied has been gently heated to make the two strands of DNA untwist, then the polymerase with the primer is added. The primer sequence of DNA has been made to be complementary to a corresponding sequence next to the gene itself. Because the primer is complementary to this sequence, it will stick to it when the DNA is warmed up and its two strands separate. In this way the primer provides a marker – a starting point for the polymerase to build onto when it starts work. The polymerase works along from the primer, building up a new strand of DNA to produce a new double spiral. When this is complete, it is warmed up, untwisted and the whole procedure is gone through again. And so on.

HOT SPRING ENZYMES SPEED UP COPYING

A further refinement, recently introduced, is to use a DNA polymerase taken from thermophilic bacteria which live in hot springs. The thermophilic enzyme is unaffected by the successive heatings required to make the strands of DNA separate. Polymerase from cells that live at ordinary temperatures is destroyed by the heating, so a fresh lot of polymerase had to be added after each warming and separation of DNA strands.

The detail is quite complex, but the important thing is simply that the enzyme, DNA polymerase, which has the natural function of copying DNA when cells divide, has been taken out of cells and can now be used to make millions of copies of any required gene, quickly and reliably. This is PCR, the Polymerase Chain Reaction.

COMBATTING CANCER AND CRIMINALS

A new use for PCR seems to appear almost every day. It has made the diagnosis of genetic defects that cause disease, in foetuses and elsewhere, much easier and more reliable. A tiny sample of tissue, if necessary even a single cell from a very early foetus, can provide enough DNA for a firm diagnosis. PCR will copy the DNA millions of times and so provide an abundance of genetic material to make the search for the defect easy.

Molecular archaeology – learning about the genes of ancient people and extinct animals – has been made possible by PCR. DNA fingerprinting, the technique invented by Professor Alec Jeffreys of Leicester University, England, has been greatly enhanced by it. Fingerprinting depends on Professor Jeffreys' discovery that there are sequences of DNA in-between genes, known as polymorphisms, which are different in every individual and so can be used to identify which person a sample of tissue came from. PCR has made it possible to amplify minute amounts of DNA in blood, the roots of single hairs, skin or semen into quantities which make the identication of individual polymorphisms easy. This helps the identification of muggers, murderers and rapists and the reliable determination of disputed family relationships.

The diagnosis of diseases including cancer has also been made much easier by PCR. A tiny amount of telltale DNA which can only have come from a virus, such as the AIDS virus, or which is clearly from a malignant cell can now be picked out, using an appropriate primer, and copied until it is easy to detect.

CHAPTER 3

GENE THERAPY

The 31st July 1990 was a landmark in the early history of genetic engineering: it was the day when an ethical committee set up by the US National Institutes of Health approved the first-ever use of gene therapy. It was approved for two purposes, to treat a deadly form of skin cancer, and a rare, also deadly, disease of the immune system that affects children. The first results from the first preliminary trials of gene therapy for the second of these uses already look encouraging. Gene therapy will probably be used to treat several diseases by the end of the century.

One of the two proposals agreed by the ethical committee involved adding genes to white blood cells, cells which form part of the immune system which defends us against disease. The aim is to make the immune cells fight cancer more effectively. Five patients suffering from melanoma, the most deadly form of skin cancer, were treated in the following way. Blood samples were taken from them and immune cells were isolated from the blood. Then extra genes were added to the immune cells, genes for a human body substance called Tumour Necrosis Factor – TNF for short. The immune cells with added genes were then injected back into the patients, into or near the site of their cancer.

The hope – and at the time of writing it is no more than a hope – is that cells with the added

TNF genes will produce extra TNF which will help the immune system to kill melanoma cancer cells. If the results are encouraging there are plans to use the same technique to try to treat other common cancers, such as those of the colon and kidney.

TREATING DOOMED CHILDREN

The other approved plan is to treat infants affected by a rare and invariably fatal childhood disease known as Severe Combined Immune Deficiency. This is caused by a defective gene. If part of a gene, even just one base, is defective or missing, then the corresponding part of the protein for which the gene codes will also be defective.

The defect responsible for combined immune deficiency affects proteins in immune cells – white blood cells which are continually formed in the

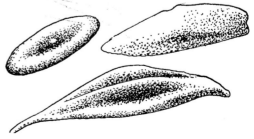

A genetic mutation produces defective haemoglobin which distorts the normally rounded blood cells in sickle cell anaemia.

marrow of the big bones of the body to replace cells as they die. The treatment planned for children affected involves sucking some of the infants' bone marrow out of a large bone with a syringe, growing the bone marrow cells in the laboratory, and then adding the correct version of the gene which is defective. When the gene has been added, the cells are grown for a while longer in the laboratory and are then re-injected back into the child.

The hope, supported by tests in animals, is that cells with added healthy genes will multiply in the bone marrow and will produce enough healthy immune cells to compensate for the defective cells produced by the bone marrow with the defective gene. If the treatment doesn't cure the condition, it may still produce a real improvement, whereas prior to gene therapy no treatment had any beneficial effect at all.

The man in charge of this research is Dr. French Anderson of the US National Institute of Health. In the week that his plan to treat Severe Combined Immune Deficiency with gene therapy was approved, he told me:

"The people we are treating are youngsters who are born without a functioning immune system. The most famous one in the country (the USA) was David the bubble boy, who lived his whole life in a bubble (a transparent membrane protecting against disease) in Houston. The genetic defect responsible for the condition is in an enzyme known as ADA, standing for Adenine DNA-ase. The youngsters have a defect in the gene for that enzyme and we hope to put a normal copy of that gene back into the immune cells of these patients."

Severe combined immune deficiency affects only a few dozen people in the world. But it was chosen as a first target for gene therapy because the condition is untreatable and invariably fatal. At the time of writing the first patient to be treated is making encouraging progress.

Defects affecting blood cells – both the white immune cells of the immune system and the red cells which carry oxygen from the lungs round the body – offer easier targets for gene therapy than any other parts of the body. This is because blood

David the Bubble Boy.

cells are made in the bone marrow, and before gene therapy was thought of, techniques had already been developed for removing the so-called stem cells of the marrow that produce new red and white cells, manipulating the stem cells in various ways, and replacing them in the bone marrow. But much more common diseases will be treated by gene therapy in the not-too distant future. As Dr. French Anderson put it to us:

"The significance of the approval for this therapy is that this disease (severe combined immune deficiency) represents a prototype, a first step. If we are successful then it opens up a broad range of diseases for gene therapy, including diabetes, sickle cell anaemia, cystic fibrosis, as well as other areas of disease such as AIDS, cardiovascular disease, and forms of cancer. This single approval is the first step to what will probably be a revolution in medical treatment over the next ten to twenty years."

VIRUSES USED IN GENE THERAPY

We have heard quite a lot now about inserting genes into cells so perhaps it is time to look at how it is done. There are several different ways. One method is already being used for human gene therapy, in order to insert human genes into human cells. The genes in human cells, like all genes, are sections of long DNA molecules coiled inside chromosomes. Because the genetic engineer wants the added genes to work just like the genes in the human cells, he wants to insert the genes right into the DNA inside the chromosomes. To achieve this he needs to cut a DNA molecule and insert an extra sequence – the added gene – between the cut ends, and join it up again.

This appeared very difficult to genetic engineers, but it is routine for some viruses. A virus is a much simpler form of life than any other. It doesn't have enough genes to make cells to live in. Instead the viral genes invade someone else's cells – yours or mine for example – and take over control of our cells as if the viral genes were our own genes.

A few of the viral genes code for one or two proteins which form protective coats around the genes, making symmetrical virus particles composed of bundles of genes inside protein coats.

Once a virus particle has got into a host cell in our bodies it multiplies fast. Many new virus particles are formed. They are made – adding insult to injury – by the enzymes of our own cells, which are brought under the control of the virus. Some viruses take control of the cell they infect by inserting their own genes, viral genes, into the DNA of the infected cell, so that the viral genes become indistinguishable from the genes of the infected cell.

This is a very clever tactic. The immune system does not recognise foreign DNA (genes) as being foreign. Only proteins are recognised as foreign. So, once the viral genes have become integrated among an infected cell's own genes, they will be treated by the infected cell exactly as if they were its own genes. Viruses have also evolved "bells and whistles" which give orders which cannot be disobeyed to the infected cells. They make the cell obey viral genes as the cell's top priority.

Most of the infected cell's resources are subverted to making new virus particles, according to the instructions of the viral genes. These genes become so integrated in among the cell's own genes that they may live there for many years, doing nothing most of the time, but occasionally switching themselves on and ordering the cell to

make more virus particles. Meanwhile the viral genes are passed on to new cells every time the infected cells divide.

Only some viruses behave like this, planting their genes right down in among the indigenous genes of the infected cells. This type of virus is known as a retrovirus. Many other viruses have genes that just float around in the outer parts of infected cells and never get into the nucleus among the cell's own genes.

(One reason for interest in retroviruses is that they include the Human Immune Viruses (HIVs for short) that cause AIDS. Without the techniques of genetic engineering, and the tricks genetic engineers can play to combat viruses, there would not be the strong hope there now is of developing a vaccine to protect people against AIDS within a few years.

If the AIDS epidemic had come twenty years earlier, before the dawn of genetic engineering, medical research would have been absolutely helpless against HIV. When the epidemic arrived, research rapidly revealed what a formidable adversary HIV was, but also pointed the way towards possible means of preventing the virus from entering cells. Research is also showing how vaccines to combat the virus may be made by genetic engineering. We will hear more about this in Chapter 7.)

Retroviruses offer an excellent means of smuggling extra genes into cells, because they do this naturally with their own genes. Genetic engineers are inserting human genes into retroviruses, and then allowing the retroviruses to infect human cells. As the retrovirus inserts its own genes naturally among the infected cell's own genes, it also inserts the added human gene.

Retroviruses are beginning to be used in this way in the first approved gene therapy projects, to insert genes for tumour necrosis factor into immune cells to fight melanoma, and other genes into bone marrow cells to try to cure severe combined immune deficiency. First, the gene to be introduced is cloned by inserting it into a fast-growing laboratory cell culture. A culture of the bacteria Eschericia coli or E. coli is usually used for this. Then the gene is inserted into a retrovirus by cutting the virus's own DNA and splicing the human gene into the cut.

More genetic engineering is needed to make the virus harmless, and this is done by snipping out the genes which make it able to reproduce. The virus is left still able to infect human cells, but no longer able to reproduce when inside them. Then the retrovirus containing the human gene is allowed naturally to infect the cells which are to be given extra genes. Finally, the cells with the added genes are replaced in the patient's body.

How Safe is Gene Therapy?

It has taken a long time, perhaps ten years of patient research, to get to the point where all this works well enough and safely enough to try on the first human patients. Extensive tests on animals have been carried out to make sure that the altered retrovirus used as a vector (the agent used to carry genes into cells) really has been rendered incapable of reproduction and can't cause a harmful infection. The doctors also have to be sure that putting extra genes into human cells won't trigger off latent oncogenes – genes which are normally harmless and beneficial, but can cause cancer if they are switched on, expressed, in the wrong place or at the wrong time, or both. (See chapter eight.)

There has been some public concern about gene therapy. Some concern, given the novelty of the technique, is understandable. Much, however, has been whipped up by scaremongers who make a living out of exploiting public fears. The truth is that in every new treatment there is a moment when the big jump from animal tests to human tests has inevitably to be made. No animal is quite like a human and so there must always be real and unavoidable risks.

This is why completely new therapies are normally first tested on people for whom no other therapy offers any hope of a cure, and why combined immune deficiency and advanced melanoma have been chosen as the first two conditions on which to test the new therapy. Much will be learned from the first tests, about how best to use gene therapy. Results from later tests will be

better than the results of the first tests.

What can also be said with confidence is that in the past other new treatments have been given for the first time with less exhaustive safety tests, greater risks of unexpected side effects, and less hope of real advances in curing people of disease than is the case with gene therapy.

Correcting Nature's Mistake's

Medicine, after all, is built on the notion that there are mistakes made in nature which we need to correct, or we wouldn't be treating people at all. What gene therapy is putting in our hands is a more effective tool to do the correction than we had before. The sufferings of many people will be ameliorated by this tool. It is not arrogance which is driving most scientists into this kind of activity, rather the exhilaration they feel at being provided with, for perhaps the first time, truly effective tools for treating disease.

It may have been noticed that the first two conditions to be treated by gene therapy – melanoma and immune deficiency – are quite different kinds of diseases. They typify the two different directions that gene therapy is likely to take. One aim is to cure diseases like immune deficiency caused by one or more genes being defective, or absent. The other is to cure or treat conditions like melanoma which are not caused by simple genetic defects, though our genes may predispose us to them.

Immune deficiency is a condition caused by an inherited defective gene. Better techniques for diagnosing genetic defects before birth, even before conception, (see chapter 4) will make it increasingly easy to prevent the births of babies affected by crippling and fatal defects, although ways to circumvent the strongest religious objections have yet to be found. But a continuing need will still remain to treat millions of people every year for diseases caused by defective genes. This is because defects continually occur spontaneously in people whose family history was unaffected by them. Muscular dystrophy is one example.

Genetic engineers hope eventually to treat and

even to cure such conditions, which are caused simply by a single defective gene. The new treatments may involve inserting enough healthy normal genes to compensate for the defective genes into whatever part of the body is affected by the defect: muscles in muscular dystrophy or bone marrow in immune system disorders, for example.

But there's more to it than simply adding good genes to compensate for bad. Once scientists have identified which gene it is that is defective and responsible for a particular disease, then they can work out, from the sequence of the bases in the gene, the exact corresponding sequence of the amino acids in the protein the gene must code for.

Each successive triplet of bases along the gene defines each successive amino acid along the corresponding chain of the protein molecule. So, once a defective gene is identified, the protein it codes for can be exactly described. Scientists can then search for that protein in the body. When they find the protein – which may take some time as there are about one hundred thousand different proteins in the human body – they can work out the actual function of the protein in the body.

It may then turn out that the best way to compensate for a defect in the gene, and a corresponding defect in the protein, is not to inject healthy genes into the parts of the body affected. It may be better to inject the protein itself, or to compensate for its absence in some other way. But doctors won't know what approach is best for each genetic disease until they know what the protein affected is, where it is and what it does. Whatever therapy is eventually used, however, it will still depend on the ability to isolate, clone and sequence genes, and on the understanding of how sequences of DNA determine the structures and functions of proteins.

More than 2,000 diseases are known to be caused by defects in single genes. As infectious diseases have been brought more and more under control, in Western countries at least, so conditions caused by genetic defects have become more and more relatively important as causes of death and ill-health. While infant mortality in the UK declined from 154 deaths per 1,000 in 1900 to 16 per 1,000 in 1984, the percentage of such deaths attributable to genetic abnormalities rose from 5% to 30%.

It is increasingly possible to identify such defects early in pregnancy, or even (though this development is at a very early stage), before fertilisation, so as to prevent the births of babies affected by genetic defects. But a large proportion of defects will always arise spontaneously through mutations (random, usually harmful changes in genes). These will always lead to the births of large numbers of people affected by genetic defects and

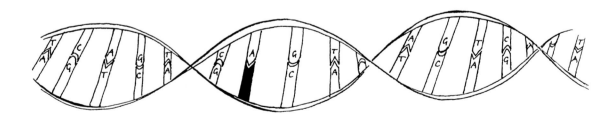

DNA showing a single gene defect which can cause diseases such as cystic fibrosis and muscular dystrophy.

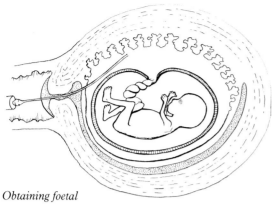

Obtaining foetal
DNA from an 8 week old foetus.

consequent illness because many such births are unpredictable.

GENE THERAPY FOR HEART DISEASE AND CANCER?

Diseases caused by single gene defects, cystic fibrosis and muscular dystrophy for example, used to be thought of as the only natural targets for gene therapy. But in the last few years, even before the development of any true human gene therapy, the inventiveness of genetic engineers has widened the horizons enormously. Now scientists are working towards the prevention by gene therapy of coronary heart disease, forms of cancer, diabetes and other very common conditions.

Though these conditions are not caused by genetic defects, genes which are inherited make people more or less susceptible to them. Several genes, each having a different effect, have been recognised as making the person possessing them more susceptible to coronary heart disease. Other genes help to protect against such disease. Doctors now hope it will be possible to help to protect people against coronary heart disease by giving them extra protective genes, using gene therapy.

So, as well as simply thinking in terms of replacing a defective gene with a good gene, rather like replacing a defective part in a car engine, genetic engineers are now thinking of using gene therapy much more like conventional drugs, but with some important potential advantages. They are planning to plug extra protective genes into people to help to guard against coronary heart disease, cancer or diabetes.

THERAPY TO LAST A LIFETIME?

One big advantage of gene therapy is going to be that the treatment will last for a lifetime. A dose of a drug lasts only for as long as it takes the human body to break down the drug chemical which has been swallowed or injected – just a few hours. But the genes used for therapy will be not drugs but blueprints for drugs, the body's natural drugs: the substances that defend us naturally against disease. Once the gene for making such a natural drug is implanted into someone (assuming the gene's bells and whistles are working properly) then the cells containing the gene, and all their daughter cells when they divide, will go on making the gene's product, the natural medicine, for life.

There are more potential advantages of gene therapy. In most parts of the body, cells with added genes will receive the myriad chemical signals which travel in the bloodstream, the signals by which the body adjusts its cells' activities to its continually varying needs. The cells will respond to the signals and their extra genes will respond too. So, with a bit of luck and the right bells and whistles, more useful substances will be produced when the body needs more, and less will be made when the body needs less.

Professor Richard Mulligan of the Massachusetts Institute of Technology (MIT), a pioneering worker in the field, says that gene therapy will first be used to treat defects of the immune system caused by genetic defects affecting the bone marrow. After bone marrow the next likely target for gene therapy, says Mulligan, is the liver. Defective genes in liver cells; hepatocytes, cause several common conditions including familial hypercholesterolaemia, in which very high levels of cholesterol accumulate in the blood, causing rapid "furring up" of the walls of arteries at an early age.

A good animal model for this condition is provided by a breed of rabbit with a missing gene, which makes rabbits affected by it die at an early age from coronary heart disease. Professor Mulligan has shown that by inserting the missing gene into no more than five percent of such a rabbit's liver cells (using the retrovirus technique described earlier) the rabbit's blood cholesterol levels can be reduced by thirty percent.

"MAJOR IMPACT" BY 2005AD

Richard Mulligan is hopeful that it may be possible to use such techniques to treat humans within the next three or four years. In ten or fifteen years he expects to see gene therapy beginning to make a major impact in medicine. But Mulligan readily agrees that it has taken several years longer to get to the point where human trials have been approved than was anticipated ten years ago. The technical problems in using retroviruses have proved tougher than expected. It has also proved difficult to ensure that the added genes induce the cells to make enough of a gene's product to be effective in treating disease.

The delay in the introduction of gene therapy has, however, provided time for inventive genetic engineers to widen their horizons. They have begun to devise ways to treat diseases which aren't caused by single gene defects. Genetic engineers have also had time to begin to bypass one of the big original problems in gene therapy. This was how to get the wanted gene into the particular part of the body where the defect has its effects. The answer, it now seems probable, will often be to implant the genes into any conveniently accessible tissue and rely upon the circulation of the blood to transport the genes' product to where it is needed.

SKIN GRAFTS WITH ADDED GENES

A team led by Professor Howard Green of the Harvard Medical School plan to try to treat dwarfism – failure to grow to normal height which is caused by deficiency of growth hormone – by using skin grafts with extra genes for growth hormone implanted. The plan, already successfully tested on mice, is to remove some skin cells from a patient with growth hormone deficiency and to inset growth hormone genes into the cells using the now familiar retrovirus technology. The cells with the added genes will then be cultured and grown in the lab until there are enough of them to provide a large skin graft. The grafters will use a technique, developed at the London Hospital, for growing a burnt patient's own skin to avoid the need for foreign grafts.

A graft about 1.8 metres in area, which is well within the state of the surgeons art, ought be enough to provide the body's growth hormone needs. The hormone would diffuse down into the blood vessels under the skin. Tests in mice show that the idea works in principle. Cells with added genes have, however, only produced growth hormone for a short time, and much less of it than is normally produced, by the pituitary gland. Louder bells and shriller whistles are clearly needed to make grafts produce enough hormone.

Using skin grafts to provide missing genes and their products is an attractive idea. The technology is well established (although growing large sheets of skin from small amounts of a patient's own tissue is only a recent achievement). If the graft fails, it's relatively easy to do another one. Professor George Brownlees of Oxford University is working towards using skin grafts in a similar way to treat Haemophilia B, one of the conditions in which blood can't clot because of a defective gene. He aims to supply the missing gene and its missing product in skin grafts. But there's a long way to go, mostly, again, in developing the right bells and whistles to attach to the genes for blood clotting factor, and so to get the skin cells to make enough of what for them is a very unfamiliar product.

Adding genes to skin grafts is one hopeful-looking way to supply missing genes and hence their products to those in need. In the further future, there's no reason why several different genes shouldn't be given to a single patient. One or two would be put in to compensate for defective genes. The others might be added for other medical purposes, to boost resistance to disease, or to supply hormones which are in short supply in old age, or to help protect against cancer or heart disease. There's no reason why all these genes should not be put into one skin graft. Each set of genes could be an individual prescription, chosen for the particular needs of a particular person.

This particular him or her may not be called a patient. In the further future he/she may be a well person who wants to be 'weller', not a sick person who wants to be made well. We use diet and exercise today to make our healthy bodies healthier. Is there any reason why, when we know how, in perhaps twenty or thirty years time, we shouldn't use gene therapy in the same way, as well as using it to cure disease?

ADDING GENES TO THE LINING OF ARTERIES

Another exciting idea being developed by at least two groups, one led by Richard Mulligan at MIT and one by Dr. Elizabeth Nabel at the University of Michigan, is to insert extra genes into the cells which line the arteries – so-called arterial endothelial cells. This form of gene therapy would have the advantage that the genes' products are poured straight into the bloodstream and carried all round the body in the blood to the places where they are needed. It has the further advantage that, because they are constantly bathed in blood being pumped past them through the artery, the cells will respond to the chemical messages carried in the blood, messages saying; "Our body needs more of this or less of that".

Already Dr. Nabel has taken endothelial cells from arteries from pigs (a simple, painless procedure, in which the pig was given an anaesthetic, a small artery near the surface of its body opened up and cells scraped from its lining) and inserted extra genes into the cells grown in the laboratory. The genes were inserted using the familiar retrovirus technique. The cells with the added genes were then put back into the lining of one of the pig's coronary arteries, using a fine flexible tube inserted into an artery in the groin and pushed up all the way to the coronary artery where the cells were squirted out of the tube onto the artery walls.

A few weeks later the coronary artery was examined to see if the added endothelial cells had settled down in its wall, and if the genes added to the cells were still being expressed. They had and they were.

The genes inserted into endothelial cells in this way so far have been "marker" genes – genes whose products aren't useful but are very easy to

detect. Now Dr. Nabel plans to insert useful genetic coding for the body's natural anti-coagulants into arterial endothelial cells. Other useful genes, genes for substances which make new blood vessels form and grow faster, or genes for substances which make arteries dilate and expand more easily to increase blood flow, could be added in the same way. They could protect against heart disease in more and more natural ways.

Someone who had had one coronary heart attack and who was known to be at risk of having another could be given some protection in this way. As with other forms of gene therapy, the potential advantage would be that, with luck, one treatment would last for life. But if it didn't, the treatment could be repeated without too much difficulty. Shoving catheters up into coronary arteries is already often done for other medical purposes. Once again, the cells with added genes will, it's hoped, respond to signals in the blood and adjust how much of their products they make according to the body's varying needs.

Endothelial cells naturally secrete products into the blood. These cells come ready equipped with the bells and whistles needed to push the products of the added genes out of the cell. This useful fact has given rise to the idea, which Richard Mulligan is very enthusiastic about, of adding genes to endothelial cells to make them produce other substances to treat other conditions quite unrelated to arteries.

Diabetes is one such example. Genes for insulin added to endothelial cells could make the cells produce insulin into the blood which would carry it to the places where it was needed. Production would respond to the body's chemical signals, make more or less insulin according to need – a big improvement on injected insulin.

SAFER ARTIFICIAL HEARTS

Arterial endothelial cells with added genes could solve another big problem – that of blood clotting in artificial blood vessels and artificial hearts. The use of mechanical pumps to help, or to take over from, the natural heart, and of artificial blood vessels to replace those lost through injury or disease, has been severely limited because blood flowing through anything other than natural blood vessels promptly starts to clot. Clots are dislodged and travel round in the blood, getting stuck in the smaller arteries including the coronary artery and arteries in the brain. This can cause strokes and permanent brain damage or coronary artery blockages and coronary heart disease.

The tendency of blood to clot when it flows through artificial arteries, or is pumped through artificial hearts, can only be countered by high doses of anti-clotting drugs, which carry their own high risks. A person taking them is like a person affected by haemophilia. When they cut themselves and have need of blood clotting, as the first essential stage in the repair of even the slightest wound, the clotting doesn't happen. This has greatly limited the use of artificial hearts and blood vessels. But Dr. Nabel hopes it may be possible to line artificial blood vessels and artificial hearts with a living coating of endothelial cells which would not cause clotting. Genes added to the cells could make them produce extra substances to prevent clotting – but not in dangerous quantities.

The heart never stops beating. Its muscle works from birth to death. It must be supplied constantly with food and oxygen. These supplies come in the blood flowing into the heart muscle through the branches of the coronary arteries. If these become narrowed by "furring up" (atherosclerosis as doctors call it) then it becomes easy for a blood clot carried along by the flow to stick in a narrowed part of the artery. This can completely cut off the blood supply to the part of the heart muscle supplied by that branch of the coronary artery. Because it never rests, and so needs a constant supply of food and oxygen, the part of the heart deprived of blood will soon die. This effect is called a coronary infarct.

PROTECTING AGAINST CORONARY ARTERY DISEASE

If the blood supply to the heart is reduced rather than completely cut off by a partial rather than a complete blockage in a branch of a coronary artery, then new branches will grow to help to compensate. This is why one of the several genes that might be put into endothelial cells in the coronary artery could be a gene for a substance that stimulates the growth of new blood vessels. Such substances and the genes for them have been identified and the genes have been cloned.

PROTECTING AGAINST STROKES

Arterial endothelial cells with added protective genes could help to protect against strokes in the same sort of way. Strokes are caused when one of the branches of the arteries supplying the brain is blocked. Deprived of food and oxygen brain cells live for only a few minutes. While they don't work as hard and constantly as heart muscle cells, brain cells have the disadvantage that before we are born they all stop dividing and never divide again. So if a bit of brain dies because the artery supplying it is blocked for more than a few minutes, we not only lose that bit of brain with all the knowledge, experience and personality it contains, we also have a very limited ability to regain what we have lost since we can't grow any new brain tissue.

Not much has yet been said about the original aim of gene therapy – to treat diseases caused by single gene defects. One reason for this is that using gene therapy for a wider range of diseases is very new and exciting. Another reason is that gene therapy for single gene defects is something which is growing out of the already well-developed medical technology used for detecting and preventing the birth of foetuses affected by single gene defects. This whole area deserves a chapter to itself.

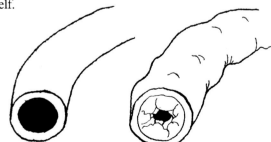

A normal and furred-up artery, showing a greatly-reduced passage for blood.

CHAPTER 4

DIAGNOSING DEFECTS BEFORE BIRTH

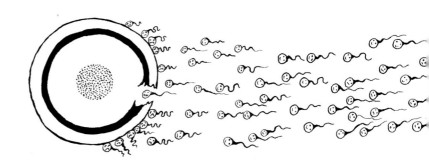

As we saw in the last chapter, while infectious diseases have come under increasing control, in the West at least, the prevalence of diseases caused by single gene defects has increased steadily. These conditions have remained untreatable by conventional drugs.

One way to attack such conditions is by developing better tests to detect the defective genes which cause conditions like cystic fibrosis, muscular dystrophy or sickle cell anaemia in a human foetus at an early stage of development. These tests can then be applied, if she so wishes, to a foetus growing in a woman who knows herself to be at risk, because she has already had one child affected by a defect, or because it "runs in the family". If the test shows the foetus carries the defective gene then the woman may request an abortion. In this way both the birth of children affected by genetic defects and the passing on of defective genes to future generations can be avoided. While widely used, these techniques are still the focus of ethical controversy.

All the tests used on foetuses used to depend upon searching for visible abnormalities, or on chemical abnormalities detected in samples from the fluid around the foetus. But it is now becoming increasingly possible to look for and detect the abnormal gene itself, if it is present. Genetic material from a tiny sample of tissue from a seven- or eight-week foetus can be tested with a DNA probe, which carries a sequence of DNA complementary to the defective form of the gene. When this is added to a sample of DNA from the foetus, the two sequences, that from the probe and that from the sample, will stick together if the foetus carries the genetic defect, but not if the foetus is normal.

Once the gene which is defective in an abnormality has been identified, the defective form of the gene can be cloned, i.e. mass-produced in cell cultures. Then copies of the defective gene can be used in DNA probes to diagnose the abnormality in a very early foetus. This has two advantages over diagnosis performed using visible or chemical defects. First, the DNA test can be performed much earlier, making a possible abortion less traumatic, and secondly, the DNA test is infallible. Either a gene is or it is not defective. The other tests tend to be only 99% or less reliable.

The techniques used to track down the genes which, when defective, cause genetic diseases, are now routine, but they take quite a long time. It has for example taken several years to pinpoint the genes which are defective in cystic fibrosis and muscular dystrophy. But even before such genes have been identified, while the hunt is still going on, it has sometimes been possible to offer a reliable genetic test, based on what are called polymorphisms. These are sequences of DNA, (not genes but sequences in between genes), which vary enormously between individuals.

Scientists have been able to identify polymorphisms which are found in only one chromosome inherited from one parent and which are also found only on the same chromosome as a defective gene. In this way polymorphisms can be and have been used to trace genetic defects down successive generations and so to diagnose a defect in a foetus even before the precise gene which is defective has been pinpointed.

PINPOINTING THE DYSTROPHIN GENE

Polymorphisms have been used increasingly to diagnose genetic defects for several years. The first big step beyond them was taken on Christmas Eve, 1987. Doctors Eric Hoffman and Lewis Kunkel of the Harvard Medical School announced they had pinpointed the gene responsible for the commonest form of muscular dystrophy, Duchenne muscular dystrophy (DMD). Since then genes involved in cystic fibrosis and several other genetic diseases have been also identified. DNA probes able to identify the defective genes in samples from foetuses have been developed. Meanwhile, having identified the gene responsible for DMD, Dr Hoffman and Dr Kunkel cloned the gene, made and analysed the protein it codes for, and christened it Dystrophin.

With the exact structure of dystrophin known, it was then possible to search for it in the human body, and to discover where it is sited in muscle. From dystrophin's location, scientists are now working out its function. When that is known – it still isn't at the time of writing, though there are theories – then scientists will be in the best possible position to try to devise ways to cure the condition. But of course doctors are at liberty to

start to try to treat DMD even before they know just how the absence of the protein which would normally be made by the missing gene affects the muscles which are weakened in DMD.

Returning to gene therapy, finding ways and designing vectors to carry the gene for dystrophin into muscle cells in people affected by DMD has been seen as a formidably difficult business. It involves the reshaping of retroviruses to make them able to perform the tricks, explained earlier, needed to get genes into cells. The retroviruses used to treat DMD will have to work not in cell cultures but in the human body. More research is needed before an approach using them will be possible. But meanwhile a remarkable discovery, made by Dr. John Wolff of Wisconsin University, may short-circuit this, properly cautious, approach and dramatically speed up the treatment of DMD, and perhaps that of many other diseases.

THE GENE SQUIRTING TECHNIQUE OF DR. WOLFF

Dr. Wolff was researching an elaborate experimental technique for gene therapy for muscle disease, in which genes were to be implanted in protective membranes into muscles. As a control for these experiments he used a deliberately crude "control" technique, in which the same genes were simply injected into muscles in a solution of water using a hypodermic syringe. The idea was that this could not possibly get the genes into the cells where they were needed in any useful quantity. In this way, the better results which were anticipated through using the elaborate approach would be thrown into relief as achieving a measure of success. But the impossible happened. To Dr. Wolff's, and every other genetic engineer's stupefaction, the control worked as well as or even better than the elaborate therapy under test.

Dr Wolff had shown that all that has to be done to insert extra genes into a useful proportion of muscle cells, of the same type as human muscle, is to load up a syringe with a solution of genes and squirt it into muscle. In the first tests about five percent of the injected genes were expressed in the muscle cells, enough for useful therapy. Dr. Wolff has already boosted the level of expression of the

The characteristics of genetic inheritance spread through 4 generations.

injected genes by simple changes to the chemical solution which is injected into the muscle. He is confident that he can raise the level of expression to that required for valuable human gene therapy.

DMD, where muscle is the tissue affected by the genetic defect, is an obvious first target for such therapy. A problem with DMD is that the dystrophin gene which is absent or defective is very large. This makes the gene very difficult to handle in complex genetic engineering procedures. Retroviruses won't easily accommodate so much extra DNA. So simply injecting a solution of dystrophin genes into the muscles of a DMD patient is a very attractive alternative. Probably by the time this book is published the idea will have been tried.

More than half the volume of a typical human body is made of muscle. So, since genes can be inserted into it reasonably easily, muscle could perhaps be used to manufacture virtually any required quantities of any body substances which are missing because of gene defects, regardless of what part of the body is affected. Repairing growth hormone deficiency is one possibility. Dr Wolff has already shown that growth hormone genes injected into muscles are expressed. He has begun to work on ways to pep up the productivity of injected genes, by tacking on more and better bells and whistles.

With such an attractively simple technique available – you mightn't even need a hospital appointment for an injection – doctors may in the future come to look at gene therapy in quite a different way. At present it is still being thought of only as a means of treating serious complaints, whether they are conditions caused by a single gene defect or conditions like coronary heart disease. If it now turns out that many conditions can be treated by injecting genes as simply – and perhaps as cheaply – as antibiotics are injected today, then gene therapy may come to be used for quite trivial complaints. A commercial company in California is already working with Dr. Wolff to exploit his discovery, calling the technique "Gene Therapeutics" to distinguish it from more elaborate gene therapy. Genes may eventually be injected for cosmetic rather than health reasons. Shall we see gene injections on offer to improve the complexion, enhance virility or to aid slimming? If they are cheap and safe, why not?

CYSTIC FIBROSIS
Muscular dystrophy has been among the first genetic disorders to have the gene responsible

identified. Progress towards gene therapy for it has gone further – though there is still a way to go – than for almost any other condition. The gene which is defective in cystic fibrosis has only very recently been identified. Scientists are now trying to devise ways to treat cystic fibrosis by gene therapy or some allied technique.

A team led by Dr Ronald Crystal at the US National Heart, Lung and Blood Institute has put the correct version of the cystic fibrosis gene into the lungs of mice, using a cold-and-sore virus as a vector. Human trials should follow in a few years.

All the time more reports are now appearing of the pinpointing of genes which are defective in various disorders. In April 1990 British, American and Polish researchers, after four years of painstaking work, located the gene which, when defective, is responsible for spinal muscular atrophies, SMAs. These are untreatable, muscle-wasting disorders which between them are the commonest causes of death from inherited gene defects in children. By the time this is published, this work will have led to a test allowing a foetus to be diagnosed as being affected by SMAs. The women involved will begin to have the option of a reliable test and, if wanted, an abortion.

In August 1990 Australian scientists announced they had found the gene which when defective causes Hunter's syndrome, another degenerative disease, which kills sufferers miserably before they reach their teens. Almost in the same week came the news that the genetic defect responsible for neurofibromatosis, a common debilitating nervous disease that affects one in four thousand children had likewise been identified, this time by United States scientists.

DETECTIVE WORK: FROM GENE TO PROTEIN

Over the next few years, more and more of the genes which cause serious diseases when they are defective will be identified. This will make it possible to make DNA probes and to diagnose the conditions infallibly in a seven- or eight-week foetus, so that early abortion can be offered. Meanwhile the ability to work out from the structure of the gene the corresponding structure of the protein which is affected by the defect, and from that to locate the protein and work out its function, will lead not only to gene therapy but also to other forms of therapy being developed. This will happen for a growing number of single gene disorders. As the functions of the proteins affected become known, it will become possible to try to devise ways to compensate for defective or absent proteins.

AVOIDING ABORTION

Abortion is an unpleasant procedure. The prospect of the repeated abortions that may have to be endured in the course of attempts to produce a child unaffected by an inherited disorder is a grim prospect. Another developing branch of biotechnology and genetic engineering is concerned with developing ingenious ways to avoid the need for even the earliest abortion.

Such techniques have been helped on their way by the creation of so-called "test-tube" babies. A women with blocked fallopian tubes (the tubes that normally carry eggs from the ovaries to the womb) can sometimes be helped to conceive by giving her drugs to make her produce extra eggs. Then several eggs are removed from her ovaries, in a very minor operation, and fertilised with her husband's sperm in a laboratory dish (not a test-tube). The fertilised eggs are allowed to grow to the stage where they have become simple microscopic balls of eight or so cells. Doctors choose the right moment to implant some of these pre-embryos, as doctors call this stage of development, in the womb.

If all goes well they will develop and be born normally. But the success rate for this procedure is still quite low, around one in five even at the most successful clinics. For this reason not only are several pre-embryos usually implanted at one go, to give the best possible chance of success, but a number are also sometimes kept alive in suspended animation in deep-freeze. This allows the option of another, later, attempt at implantation if the first attempt fails, without the need to take more eggs from the woman.

This technique has allowed many hundreds of

women who would otherwise have been childless to have babies normally. But it has also led to some ethical problems. Suppose the first attempt at implantation succeeds and the woman in question gives birth to triplets, then she won't want any more children. What happens to the pre-embryos waiting in the freezer?

DO PRE-EMBRYOS HAVE SOULS?

One option is to use them for research, to help raise the success rate of the procedure. Many object to this. Or they can be given to another woman who cannot produce eggs of her own, to enable her to give birth to a child – even though the child won't have her genes. Some people object to that. Or they can be destroyed. To some that is a form of murder. Although the pre-embryos are only featureless balls of eight or so cells, to those such as Roman Catholics who believe that the soul enters the body at the moment of fertilisation, when a genetically new individual is created, destroying a pre-embryo is tantamount to murder.

This is not a book about test-tube babies. But the techniques developed to fertilise human eggs outside the body (in vitro fertilisation is the scientific name), and for growing pre-embryos in the laboratory, can also be used to try to avoid the birth of babies with defective genes and consequent disease. One way to prevent such births is to use DNA probes to test a seven- or eight-week foetus and then to offer abortion if the foetus has the defect. Another way is to go through the whole in vitro fertilisation procedure: fertility drugs, removing several eggs, fertilising them all and growing them to pre-embryos, and then to test the pre-embryos for the defect.

Doctors at the Hammersmith Hospital in London reported in April 1990 that if just one or two cells are removed from a pre-embryo and tested with DNA probes to see if the pre-embryo carries a defective gene, and the embryo is found not to be deficient, it will go on and develop normally when reimplanted in the womb. Sometimes all that is necessary is to determine the sex of the pre-embryo, since some defects only occur in one or the other sex. The removal of cells

for testing doesn't damage the pre-embryo. Its chances of survival will be as good as those of an embryo from which no cells were removed. The removal of the cells doesn't affect the embryo's development in any way.

This technique offers an alternative to abortion which many women will find preferable as it becomes more widely available. Although minor surgery to remove eggs is necessary, and the chance of a successful pregnancy is only one in four at best, this may still be preferable to repeated pregnancy, foetal testing and perhaps repeated abortion.

To Catholic theologians, however, the testing and destruction of a pre-embryo because it carries a genetic defect is a form of abortion. In Catholic theology the soul has already entered the body of a new individual, who is formed when the egg from which the pre-embryo grew was fertilised. Cardinal Hume, the Catholic Archbishop of Westminster, has described legislation permitting research on pre-embryos as "the abandoning of fundamental aspects of Christian morality". For this and other reasons two leaders in research in this field, Dr. Marilyn Monk and Dr. Cathy Holding of the Mammalian Development Research Unit in London, have developed a technique which makes it possible to detect some genetic abnormalities at least in an egg before fertilisation.

DETECTING ABNORMALITIES BEFORE FERTILISATION

In Chapter One we saw how eggs are formed, by a reduction division, in which the double set of chromosomes in all living cells is reduced to a single set in the egg. The other product of each reduction division is called a polar body. When an egg is formed in an ovary the polar body formed at the same time remains close to the egg. One of each pair of genes in the cell which underwent the reduction division ends up in the egg. The other member of the pair ends up in the polar body.

I said earlier that genetic defects are usually carried only on one member of a pair of genes. If this is so then, at the reduction division, the defective member of the pair will end up either in

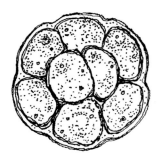

The 8 cells of a pre-embryo.

the polar body or in the egg. If the polar body is tested for the defect and the defect is found, then that means the egg doesn't carry a defect, and no further tests are needed. The egg can be fertilised in the dish, grown to a pre-embryo and implanted without further tests. If on the other hand, the polar body is tested and found not to carry the defect, then that means the egg must have the defect. So the egg isn't fertilised and is destroyed.

No religious objection to that procedure is anticipated, because no-one maintains that an unfertilised egg is a person. It can't be, because half the person-to-be's genes, half his or her inherited characteristics, haven't arrived yet. They come in the sperm. During her lifetime, a woman's body will naturally discard hundreds of unfertilized eggs through menstruation.

Polar body testing may soon offer an acceptable alternative for people of some religious persuasions to forbidden abortion on the one hand, or the birth of doomed children on the other. Dr. Marilyn Monk has already shown that the test works for sickle cell anaemia and thalassaemia, two of the most common conditions caused by inherited genetic defects.

Techniques for avoiding the birth of babies with genetic defects depend upon the development of techniques for identifying, isolating and cloning genes, just as much as do techniques for trying to cure such defects when people carrying them are born. Regardless of religious beliefs, gene therapy as well as the elimination of defective genes will always be needed, because unpredictable defects, and even completely new defects, will keep cropping up.

Two Kinds of Gene Therapy

At this point it is important to make a distinction between two possible kinds of gene therapy. All the ideas we have talked about so far involve what is called somatic gene therapy. This involves attempts to cure someone's disease by adding extra genes which will, hopefully, compensate for defective genes or perhaps for some condition not caused by defective genes for that person's life time.

Those extra genes will have no effect whatever on that person's descendants. Because the genes are not being put into the person's testes or ovaries, they won't go into sperms or eggs, and so the extra genes won't go on to the next generation. New genes will be put, as we have heard, into arteries, skin grafts, muscles and other parts of the body, but not into the cells which form sperms and eggs. So the effects of added genes die when the person they are put into dies. That is somatic gene therapy.

Somatic Gene Therapy Approved

Objections to somatic gene therapy are, doctors agree, really based on confusion and ignorance. This kind of therapy is only just getting under way, later than expected, because of technical problems and the need to meet very tough safety standards. But somatic gene therapy will help doctors to treat many common as well as rare conditions, including many not caused by genetic defects, in new and better ways. Somatic gene therapy will be less hazardous even at the start than many other new treatments, which offered lesser potential benefits when they were started. People who think there is something specially dangerous about somatic gene therapy either don't understand it at all, or are muddling it up with the other possible kind of gene therapy, germ line gene therapy.

Germ Line Germ Therapy

Germ line gene therapy, if it were undertaken, would involve adding genes to the reproductive organs, or to very early embryos. Thus the added genes would be passed on to the next generation.

Animal experiments have already shown that if

genes are added to sperms or eggs before fertilisation, or to pre-embryos at a very early stage of development, then these added genes will be present in every cell of the person who grows from the fertilised egg or pre-embryo. That includes the reproductive cells. So the added genes will be handed on to future generations.

At present all scientists and doctors are emphatic that they will not attempt germ line gene therapy in humans. They regard it as absolutely immoral to tamper with the genes of future generations, even in a good cause. And – at present – there is really no reason why anyone should want to attempt germ line gene therapy. The best way to get rid of genetic defects and consequent diseases is not to add in good genes but to screen out bad ones, in the ways already described. If that hasn't been possible and a person is born with defective genes, then therapy will try to compensate by adding the correct genes to the part of the body affected, not to the reproductive cells.

However, as we shall see in chapter eleven, veterinary scientists are already adding genes to farm animals in ways which ensure the genes are handed on to future generations. This is being done for a variety of purposes, one of which is, or soon will be, to make the animals more resistant to disease. Added genes may for example make sheep resistant to a disease like AIDS and chickens resistant to pneumonia.

As the techniques needed to add genes to animals become established and are shown to be simple, safe and reliable, it seems likely that eventually (which probably means in less than fifty years time) people will become aware of it. They will also become aware that only the unwillingness of scientists to tamper with the genes of generations yet unborn is preventing them from endowing their children and their children's children with natural resistance to some nasty diseases. It will be clear from work with animals that this could be done by a simple procedure, involving the insertion of the wanted gene into the reproductive organs of mothers and fathers who, like so many, are determined to get the best of everything for their children.

"PLAYING GOD"WITH FUTURE GENERATIONS

It seems to me that this is when some of the real arguments about whether humans should "Play God" will begin. As I've said, my own bet (mine because, when I've tried to discuss these future issues with other people including scientists I've usually found they haven't looked that far ahead) is that, once animal work has shown adding genes to future generations is safe and it works, then people will demand it for their families. And eventually, being in a majority, they'll get it.

By the time we know enough about genes for it to be feasible for people soberly to consider investing in extra genes for their families' future, as we invest in property and higher education today, I suspect public attitudes to genetic engineering will have undergone a massive change. No terrible disaster will have happened. The benefits which are only just beginning to show today will be popping up all over the place. AIDS will have been controlled by vaccines and perhaps by drugs that could never have been made without genetic engineering and the public will know it. The great tropical parasitic diseases will at last be in retreat; the tide against them will be turned by vaccines which could only have been made by genetic engineering, and the public will know it.

New and better treatments for heart disease and forms of cancer, only possible through genetic engineering, will have come along, and the public will know where they come from. Chemical industry will be more efficient, cleaner and "greener", all though biotechnology based in the end on genetic engineering, and the companies using it won't fail to tell the public. Maybe agriculture will have benefited more than anything. Overall the doubts and fears that hang over genetic engineering will have blown away.

BUYING BETTER GENES

This is all only informed guesswork. The pace of research alters unpredictably, and the benefits that come from it are seldom quite what one expects. But they come. It may be that in fifty years time the medical establishment will be seen as fuddy-duddy and secretive in holding back the rewards of research from the public. People will clamour to buy the genes that, by then, scientists will have proved can make children not only healthier but cleverer and taller and stronger and more beautiful.

By then, or perhaps even sooner, science will have gone well beyond just being able to combat disease with genes. Genetic engineers will know quite a lot about how to improve on nature. If we want it, we'll be able to take on some of the powers that today many believe should belong only to God or to Nature (seen this time as a benevolent entity) – but not to Man.

We are not the product of our genes alone. Every grandmother who has seen two generations of children knows that. But she also knows how powerful genes are. We are going to discover how to plug new genes into our descendants. That won't alter the fact that, as we grow up, it is not just our genes but the interplay between our potential, determined by our genes, and the environment around us, especially our family environment, that determines our abilities and our characters. But science will have revealed genes that can give the family possessing them advantages in life.

Should such genes be available to everyone or just to those with money to pay for them? Families with high intelligence and disease resistance will be national assets. But if nations can't afford to give the genes for them to everyone, then who should be chosen? Will the expensive ability to improve human genetic stock widen the gap between rich and poor nations as well as between rich and poor people? How far should people be allowed by law to change themselves and their descendants by adding in genes? Should it go beyond disease resistance, to intelligence? Or strength? What about sporting contests? Or beauty?

There has been great public interest in the news that genetic engineers have changed the sex of a mouse, by implanting the single gene now known to be responsible for male sex into a female pre-embryo. While it is already possible to choose the sex of a human child, by examining pre-embryos and implanting only the wanted sex, this manipulation was a shock demonstration of the power of genetic engineering.

To make informed decisions of such matters the public will need to understand genetic engineering much more than it does now. We are not confronted with these issues yet (though ethical issues over human genes are beginning to emerge). But if through fear and ignorance any public in the next few years simply turns its back on genetic engineering and says "I want none of this", then later on the vital choices, the great decisions, will still be made. They will just be made somewhere else, by nations that have gone on to develop the skills and make the decisions.

I have dwelt on the ethics of germ line therapy and, in the future, what might be called genetic enhancement, because there is a lot of confusion about the distinction between this and somatic gene therapy. I must repeat that, while I've speculated about a not-too-distant future in which germ line therapy and enhancement may be used, and when we will know a great deal more about genes, and when public attitudes may have changed drastically, scientists today are even more opposed to any use of germ line therapy than are the public at large. The fifth summit conference on Bioethics, in 1988, concluded that germ line therapy should not be considered at all (while endorsing somatic gene therapy, and concluding it needed only the same safeguards as any other new therapy). And all the European Medical Research Councils, in 1988, jointly declared that inserting genes in the human germ line (reproductive cells) should not even be contemplated.

RETHINKING GERM LINE THERAPY

My suggestion is that germ line therapy, responsibly undertaken for good medical reasons, may eventually be regarded as acceptable, but only in the distant future. That may be too cautious. At the 1991 meeting of the American Association for the Advancement of Science, Leroy Walters, Director of the Centre for Bioethics in Georgetown University in Washington, said: "The time is ripe for a detailed public discussion of the ethical issues surrounding germ line genetic

The Embryo 'Supermarket'.

intervention in humans." He added that animal work had already shown the potential for the technique.

Leroy Walters also quoted a declaration by participants from 24 nations at a July 1990 meeting of the Council for International Organisations of Medical Sciences, which, speaking of germ line therapy said: "...such therapy might be the only means of treating certain conditions and therefore continued discussion of both its technical and its ethical aspects is essential...(though) its safety must be very well established."

According to Professor Walters, it may eventually be possible to develop techniques to replace defective cells forming sperms and egg with healthy cells, so that people under the shadow of producing defective foetuses could have that shadow removed. Genetic engineering able to delete defective genes in testes and ovaries and replace them with healthy genes, with 100% reliability, is well in the future. But he also said that in his view it was "not too early to intensify and broaden the discussion of germ line gene intervention, even if the fruits of current research efforts become apparent only in the 21st century."

PRE-EMBRYO SUPERMARKETS

Adding genes to germ lines is only one new technology which may come into being for improving one's children. Today donor eggs or donor pre-embryos are being used to give women who can't produce eggs of their own, or who know their own offspring would carry deadly genetic defects, the chance to bear healthy children. Tomorrow the same technology could be used by perfectly healthy women, who just want a baby with a superior genetic endowment. In very liberal societies, women may eventually be able to choose pre-embryos from a kind of classy embryo supermarket, where thousands of pre-embryos would be stored, indexed with details of the appearance and genetic traits and abilities of their genetic parents. It is not unreasonable to suppose that prospective parents, perhaps especially single women, will wish to choose the genes of their offspring with great care, given the opportunity. In a hundred years time the combination of donor eggs and the ability to insert genes into pre-embryos could enable an embryo supermarket to offer pretty well any desired combination.

GENES FOR CANCER AND HEART DISEASE

As well as the ethical issue of which genes we should be allowed to add to our offspring, there is the parallel issue of which genes we should be allowed to get rid of. Several genes are now known which in different ways predispose to heart disease and cancer. If parents ask doctors for tests to identify foetuses with such genes, and ask for abortions if the genes are there, should doctors agree? Surely not; a bigger chance of getting a killer disease is a very different thing from the certainty of dying from a genetic defect. But perhaps doctors should consider abortion for those foetuses who are quite disastrously susceptible to heart disease, which have all the six or seven known "bad" genes? Where should they draw the line?

There is bound to be more pressure to abort for a wider variety of genetic susceptibilities, as well as genetic defects. But there will also be a movement the other way. As more and more diseases caused by genetic diseases become curable by somatic gene therapy, Catholic and some other doctors will be increasingly unwilling to abort foetuses affected by such defects. If such conditions aren't screened out by abortion, but are instead cured in adulthood by somatic gene therapy, then the defect responsible for them will spread and spread, in a way that in the past has been prevented, because people affected by such defects would seldom have lived to reproduce.

Therapy Could Spread Genetic Disease

Somatic gene therapy won't eliminate genetic defects, it will only compensate for them. If a man or woman is cured of a disease caused by a genetic defect by inserting "good" genes, the insertion of the defective gene is still there in his or her testes or ovaries, in cells which divide to form eggs or sperms. So the defect will go on to the next generation, unless every pregnancy is screened using one of the techniques described earlier.

Ethical Problems

Several genes which make us more or less liable to cancer or heart disease are now known. Suppose in the future a young man from a family with a history of heart disease goes to his doctor and on to a clinic and has a blood test. He is presented with a genetic profile which says, "You have six out of seven 'bad' genes for coronary heart disease, genes which make you susceptible to it."

That's good news because the young man can do a lot to reduce his risks; by exercise, stopping smoking, losing weight, dieting and maybe, in a few years time, having some "guardian genes" implanted into his arteries or injected into his muscle. But now suppose his girlfriend demands a copy of his genetic profile and then says she won't marry him? Suppose his new employer demands a copy and then says he won't employ him? And his building society? And his insurance company? And his driving school? Should they all have a right to that gene profile? Will people be compelled to have gene tests whether they want them or not?

These questions are posed by a test (developed a few years back, dependent on DNA polymorphisms, as described earlier) for a condition called Huntington's Chorea, which is caused by a genetic defect. It causes a very unpleasant, rapidly progressive and incurable mental deterioration that doesn't start till middle age. Should those at risk, people who come from families where Huntingtons Chorea has occurred, be compelled to be tested for the condition? Should marriage partners, insurance companies, employers, have the right to demand the test? As more tests for such conditions become available, as is happening, more and more such questions will have to be answered.

So far, we have looked at the growing number of human genetic diseases that are now being pinned down to specific genes, and at the way in which this is allowing doctors to prevent and, soon, hopefully to cure such conditions. And we have looked at the problems these great achievements are bringing with them. But detecting and eliminating, or compensating for defective genes is only one medical use for genetic engineering. There is another use that may prove even more important.

This is the ability to identify the human genes for the substances – our bodies' own natural drugs, that defend us against disease every moment of the day without our knowing it. And then to use these genes, cloned outside our bodies, to make their products so they can be used like other drugs, to reinforce our natural defences when they are not strong enough. The new generation of drugs that are being produced in this way are the subject of the next chapter.

SUPERDRUGS FOR THE 21ST CENTURY

Killer cells attacking a virus.

Our bodies are defended by a complex army of cells, the cells of the immune system. These immune cells are given their orders to attack invading microorganisms; bacteria, viruses and parasites, by chemical signals. Each signal is produced by one set of immune cells, travels through the bloodstream, and is received by others. The signals sent by immune cells are called interleukins. The genes for interleukins are now one by one being identified and cloned, allowing the interleukins to be made outside the body by cell cultures and tested as drugs. They are already being used medically to try to stimulate the immune systems of sick people to combat their diseases more strongly.

NATURAL KILLER CELLS ATTACK CANCER

This kind of therapy is being used for cancer patients by Dr. Stephen Rosenberg of the US National Institute of Health. Dr. Rosenberg has taken immune cells which fight cancer from cancer patients with inoperable cancers, sometimes selecting immune cells from inside tumours, since these are the cells which are attacking the cancer most strongly. He has treated these cells outside the body of the patient with an interleukin, Interleukin-2 or IL-2 for short, which can now be made outside the body.

IL-2 has the known effect of transforming ordinary immune cells into what are called Natural Killer or NK cells. NK cells attack cancer tumours more immediately and more savagely than any other immune cells. The cells made into NK cells in this way are injected back into the tumour. Finally more IL-2 is injected into the patient, to keep the newly-created NK cells up to the mark, and to stimulate more immune cells in the patient's body to behave like NK cells and attack the cancer.

Interleukins are also known as lymphokines. At the time of writing, this technique – the use of Lymphokine-Activated Killer cells or LAK cells as they are called for short – has given encouraging

INHERITANCE OF CYSTIC FIBROSIS

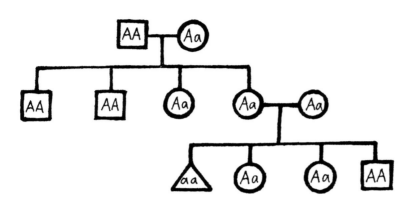

This genetic family tree shows how cystic fibrosis, or any genetically inherited disease, can be passed on unless future genetic engineering techniques can identify and treat the defective gene.

results in Phase I trials. That means that when it was used in patients who had failed to respond to other treatments, some improvement was seen. Further, large-scale, Phase 2 trials will be carried out (and will probably be completed by the time this is published). In Phase 2 doctors will have learnt from the first tests how to use the therapy to get the best results.

SIDE-EFFECTS OF POTENT LYMPHOKINES

So far eight lymphokines have been identified and the genes for them cloned, making it possible to investigate their effects outside the human body and to discover whether they can be used as medical drugs. At the time of writing, three lymphokines are undergoing clinical trials and three more are undergoing preliminary tests on patients. It is already clear that lymphokines have far more potent effects on the human body than conventional drugs, because they act on living cells through specialised receptors, which amplify their effects. But those effects are numerous and complex, not simple and single.

Whether lymphokines become, as many hope, the most important class of medical drugs by 2000 AD, will depend very much on whether they can

be chemically modified to reduce their unwanted effects while retaining the potency of the wanted effects.

Other natural human body substances besides lymphokines are now being produced outside the body and used or tested as drugs, as the genes for them are identified and cloned. The first and still the most famous such substance to be cloned and used as a drug was interferon. Three different forms of interferon are now known, alpha, beta and gamma, each with different effects. All are being used, with limited though real success to treat cancers and other diseases.

AIDS AND CANCER TREATMENT

Another promising group of human body control substances now being cloned and tested as drugs are the Colony Stimulating Factors or CSFs, which naturally stimulate selected groups of cells in the body to grow and divide more rapidly. CSFs are being tested as drugs used to stimulate the bone marrow of AIDS patients and cancer patients undergoing chemotherapy, who have reduced populations of immune cells, to work overtime to produce extra immune cells to help to make up the deficiency. Erythropoietin, which stimulates the production of red blood cells, is being used very successfully in a similar way to step up the production of red cells by the bone marrow.

HELPING WOUNDS HEAL

Then there are the growth factors, a group of substances each of which stimulates cells of a different part of the body; skin cells, muscle cells or fibroblasts (connective tissue cells), to grow and divide. Fibroblast growth factor, in particular, has already been used to speed up the formation of new blood vessels and to help wounds to heal. It may soon be used applied in ointments to hasten the healing of burns, ulcers and bedsores.

Human growth hormone is a different substance, with more generalised effects than the growth factors. Until a few years ago, growth hormone could only be extracted in tiny amounts from the pituitary glands of aborted foetuses. Now it can be made in relatively large quantities, by cloning the gene for growth hormone in cell cultures. Cloned growth hormone is now routinely used to treat dwarfs.

PROLONGING YOUTH

Recently (June 1990) some remarkable results published in the USA have suggested that growth hormone can act as a drug to prolong youth. Men between the ages of 61 and 81 who were given injections of growth hormone three times a week for six months lost fourteen percent of their body fat. The weight of their muscles, bones and internal organs went up nine percent and the thickness of their skin by seven percent. In this way the mens' physiques returned to what they had been ten or even twenty years before. Tests of growth hormone at other centres, including St. Thomas' hospital in London are now planned, by doctors who believe that, as growth hormone becomes widely available thanks to gene cloning, it may be possible to improve the quality of life for many old people by giving them daily injections. There will doubtless be side effects. For example the injections may increase the risk of arthritis, heart disease or diabetes. And they won't affect brain tissue, because brain cells don't divide and

grow after birth. So growth hormone treatment won't counteract senility, nor failing eyesight or hearing.

But if just one cloned hormone can have such substantial, though partial, rejuvenating effects, one is bound to ask as more hormones and other human body control substances are cloned, how long will it be before a cocktail of such substances, given as regular injections, or perhaps in a longer-lasting form via gene therapy, becomes available to confer a startling degree of rejuvenation – at a price. At present one year's course of growth hormone treatment for one man costs $14,000. Older people will undoubtedly be prepared to pay a lot to stave off old age for a few more years.

The problem at the moment is that, once the course of treatment is stopped, the aging process is accelerated in a few weeks to the stage of ageing the patient would have reached naturally in the time he was taking the hormone treatment. Like the most horrifying science fiction story, it is theoretically possible at the moment to age several years in as few weeks. But growth hormone is still likely to be made available on a large scale in the West. But will the developing world be able to afford such luxuries?

Another possible approach to rejuvenation comes from Switzerland, where two scientists, Englishman John Sheppard and Swiss Walter Gehring of Basle University, have prolonged the lives of fruit flies by forty percent simply by adding an extra gene to the flies, the gene for a protein known as EF 1-Alpha. Just what EF 1 Alpha does is still unknown. But it is known to be needed if cells are to be able to produce other new proteins. A growing deficiency of EF 1 Alpha with age is one apparent cause of the deterioration and eventual death of individual cells, so it may be a part cause of the deaths of all living creatures, including ourselves as well as flies. The beauty of the experiment is that it is the healthy phase of the life cycle that is prolonged, rather than merely preventing old and sick organisms from dying.

Could gene therapy do the same for humans? Could another thirty years of healthy life be sandwiched in between our thirties and our forties, say? We don't have the knowledge to try to do it now. Fruit flies (on which a great deal of genetic research has been done, because their salivary glands conveniently contain enormous and easy-to-study chromosomes) have a good many genes in common with us. But the genes which control

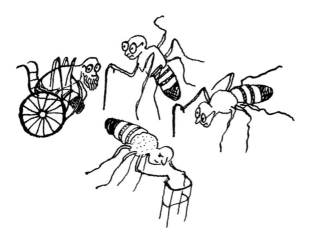

Aging fruit flies.

ageing in human cells have not yet been identified. They are probably different from those in flies.

On the other hand, it is striking that in what is still the prehistory of molecular genetics, our understanding of how genes work inside cells has already given us the ability to extend the lives of flies by forty percent, and the ability markedly to rejuvenate ourselves by the use of simple hormones.

IMMORTALITY?

The pace of such discoveries certainly suggests that we should be able to prolong life, and not just life but healthy life, in the not too distant future. But experts on the ageing process don't believe it will be possible to take a step beyond that, and to create human beings who are potentially immortal so long as they are protected against disease and accident.

As our mastery over our genes increases,

eventually we may be able to design a potentially immortal creature, similar to us in its brain power and perhaps in its outward appearance. But this would be a new creature, assembled in the unimaginable laboratory of a biotechnologist of perhaps 2090AD. It wouldn't be a modified man. Ageing and death are just too programmed into our cells and our entire selves to be programmed out without destroying the whole organism. Or so it seems at present.

A complete list of all the natural human body substances that are now being cloned and tested as drugs, or will soon be tested as drugs would be tedious, and quickly out of date. Genetic engineers are continuously identifying more of the substances that defend us, making them outside the body and testing them to see what functions they have and how they might be used as drugs. But genetic engineers are also creative people and their ideas range beyond simply manufacturing the body's natural defenders to work as drugs.

AT LAST A COLD CURE

Take that universal nuisance, the common cold. A vaccine can't economically be made to protect against it, because any one of over 100 different viruses can cause colds. It would cost too much to put them all in a vaccine to protect against such a relatively trivial complaint. But genetic engineering offers a hope of stopping colds in their tracks, and even perhaps of protecting against ever catching one, in a different way.

Dr. Stephen Markin of Boehringer Ingelheim Pharmaceuticals in the USA has cloned a gene not from a cold virus but from the receptor, the specialised region on the surfaces of the cells of the lining of the nose, through which cold virus particles get in to infect the cell. If you imagine a virus particle as a key and the receptor as a lock, you have quite a good image of what happens. It really is the exact three-dimensional shape of the virus particle fitting the shape of the receptor like a key in a lock that allows the virus to get in. If you ask why our cells should have gone to the trouble to evolve receptors to allow nasty viruses to get into them, the answer is that they didn't. Receptors

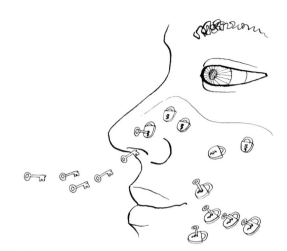

Blocking the common cold virus.

are there to allow chemical signals which tell cells how to behave in accordance with the body's needs to get in or out. Viruses have evolved to take advantage of these handy trap-doors in through the otherwise hard-to-pentrate outer membranes of the cells they infect.

Some receptors are small enough for a single gene to represent the blueprint for making them. Dr. Markin has cloned the gene for the cold virus receptor, which means he has millions of copies of the gene in cell cultures, producing millions of copies of the receptor itself, millions of copies of the "lock" through which cold virus particle "keys" get into cells. His plan is to put millions of cold virus receptors made in this way into a nasal spray, and to see if the spray can help to protect against infection with colds, and against the development of colds that have just started.

This will happen, if it happens, because a cold virus particle doesn't just nip into a cell through a receptor. It sticks in the receptor and semi-reacts with it. The hope is that virus particles entering a nose which has been sprayed with receptors will mostly find their way into, and attach themselves to, the cloned receptors in the spray, rather than the real receptors in the cells lining the nose – just because there are so many of the cloned receptors.

As Steve Markin put it to me: "We've actually used genetic engineering techniques to tailor-make a mimic of the molecule, the receptor the virus uses to attach to the cell. This molecule is in essence a decoy. When mixed in with the virus, the virus particle will bind to the decoy instead of binding to cells."

The same idea is being worked on to try and stop several other viruses, including the Human Immune Virus that causes AIDS, from entering and infecting cells. (See chapter seven). But there are problems to be overcome. Receptors are really there to receive vital chemical signals. If the nose or any other part of the body is swamped with cloned receptors acting as decoys to mop up virus particles, then the cloned receptors may also mop up the messages that should be going into the real receptors and telling cells what to do. Failure to receive such messages could cause serious illness.

There is another potential problem. Normally the immune system regards receptors as part of the body its job is to protect. If millions of copies of a receptor are made and injected into the body, then the immune system may decide that this must mean that the receptor is a foreign substance and should be attacked. The cloned receptors would then be destroyed by the immune system, before they could mop up the virus.

There might also be a much more serious side-effect. Once the immune system had decided to regard receptors of the type injected as foreign, it would attack the natural receptors on the surfaces of cells, as well as the artificially made and injected receptors. In the course of trying to cure a minor complaint, a cold, the body of the person in question would then have acquired a much more serious condition. In this vital part of the body, a receptor needed for the reception of essential signals would have been destroyed by the immune system as though this vital part of the body were part of an invading micro-organism.

These are good examples of the kinds of hazards genetic engineers and doctors developing new therapies have to watch out for. No doubt there will be occasions when, in spite of every effort, some such unexpected side effect arises which couldn't be foreseen. And people will suffer and even die because of it. It can happen in spite of every possible precaution, with any kind of new therapy. It is one reason why even the biggest pharmaceutical companies are increasingly loathe to invest huge sums in several years of research to develop completely new therapies. The more original the therapy, the greater the likelihood that unforeseeable side effects may lead to colossal losses through lawsuits. But without such risks for a few patients, the first to receive the new drug, who are anyhow usually people who can't benefit from any other treatment, there can be no major medical advances.

SUPERBLOOD

Scientists have developed a blood substitute made by genetic engineering which is safer to use than any other artificial blood. It will be several years before the new blood substitute will be ready for wide use, but tests have already shown its potential advantages, though it only performs one of the many functions of blood, that of carrying oxygen round the body.

Dr. Gary Stetler and his colleagues of the US biotechnology company Somatogen in California have made an improved form of the red substance that carries oxygen round the human body, haemoglobin, and shown it can be used as a complete substitute for blood as an oxygen carrier. Gary Stetler gave his reasons why blood substitutes are needed. First among them, he says, is the avoidance of any risk of contracting AIDS. "Probably the reason that appeals most to us is the elimination of the risk of contracting blood-borne disease from real blood transfusions. But others that are of equal importance are problems with long term storage of whole blood, problems involved with its cross matching and typing, as well as the occurrence of sudden shortages of blood during times of national emergencies, when there are large accidents, and that kind of thing."

For meeting the first aid needs caused by natural and human catastrophes such as earthquakes, plane and train crashes and, of course, war, blood substitutes would be easier to store and deploy than blood itself. Dr. Stetler's team have taken the two genes that are the

blueprints for making the two halves of the big human haemoglobin molecule, and put these genes into yeast. The yeast made a haemoglobin almost identical to human haemog
problems, however. Witho
blood cell which haemoglo
the haemoglobin made b
enough oxygen round the
cells make enough of it. I
has solved these problems.

"What we've done is co
chemically the human h
expression in these microo
the genes so that the pr
higher quantities than the
identical to the human gen
the yeast haemoglobin bett
We've altered it so that it
oxygen per gram of h
haemoglobin that you wo
blood cell. That was neces
oxygenation of tissues."

Now the genetically er
which actually performs be
and might be nickna
undergoing rigorous safety
passed as safe to use then it
use by 1995.

PIGS = HUMAN BLOOD DO

A U.S. biotech company
pursuing another approa
haemoglobin genes into p
regular haemoglobin donor
though again exhaustive sa
before it can be used on a l

AUTO-IMMUNE DISEASE

As we've seen, the imm
mistake and attack part o
defends, as if that part of
invading microorganism.
remarkably, almost m
differentiating between self, which is its own body, and not-self, which is everything else which has no business to be in its body. But mistakes are made.

Beta (killer) cells developing in the pancreas.

Occasionally, the human immune system attacks some bit of the body it is part of. This causes diseases called auto-immune diseases – diseases in which the immune system is auto-directed, mistakenly directed against self.

Genetic engineering and allied skills in biotechnology are now making it possible, for the first time ever, to investigate and understand such illnesses. Based on this new understanding, new treatments are being planned. But it should be said that they have not yet been tried in humans, and doctors will need to be sure that such treatments can't cause the kinds of problems described early with the common cold treatments.

DIABETES

A good example is one form of diabetes, juvenile onset or Type I diabetes, which affects about 15% of all diabetics. For some years, scientists have known that type I diabetes is an auto-immune disease. It's caused when the immune system of the person involved mistakenly attacks the part of the pancreas, the so-called beta cells, which normally produce insulin.

In June 1990 three teams of researchers in different countries jointly published research which showed that mice with a condition which very closely models juvenile onset diabetes could be cured by implanting extra genes into them. The implanted genes somehow switch off the harmful auto-immune reaction. It will be a long way from

this to any kind of new therapy, let alone gene therapy, for human diabetes. But the mouse experiments show it is feasible.

RHEUMATISM AND MULTIPLE SCLEROSIS

Rheumatoid arthritis and multiple sclerosis, too, are auto-immune diseases. Multiple sclerosis is caused by the immune system mistakenly attacking parts of the sheaths of nerves, made of a substance called myelin. Rheumatoid arthritis is caused by a similar reaction against the material which lines the insides of the joints of limbs. Genetic engineering and allied techniques are making it possible to identify the precise auto-immune reactions causing these conditions, and to begin to devise experimental strategies to try to prevent them.

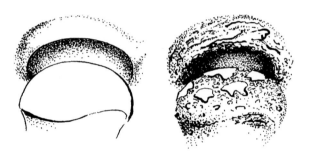

How the lining of an arthritic joint disintegrates.

In multiple sclerosis, for example, it seems likely that relatively small groups of immune cells are responsible for the harmful destruction of myelin. By identifying the groups of cells responsible, and making vaccines from killed cells of just these types, it may be possible to stimulate the immune system of a multiple sclerosis sufferer to attack and destroy just the groups of immune cells responsible for the condition, without affecting the rest of the immune system. This could eliminate the harmful reaction while leaving the immune system more or less intact to do its job of defending against disease. The idea has been tested in animals with encouraging results, but human tests are years away.

CHAPTER 6

ANTIBODIES: IMMUNITY'S GUIDED MISSILES

So far we have seen how some diseases can be treated by implanting extra genes into people, and how substances that naturally defend the human body can now be made outside the body, so as to use them as medical drugs. There is a third way in which our natural defences can be reinforced through biotechnology and genetic engineering. This is by using antibodies, the human body's first line of defence against disease. Antibodies, like interleukins and hormones, can now be made outside the body for medical and other purposes. But the way it's done is a bit different.

HOW ANTIBODIES WORK

When a virus particle or a bacterium gets into your body, a key part of your immune system's attack upon this invader will be the production of an antibody against it. If you have been infected by the virus before, your immune system will "remember" the infection. Antibodies will be being produced within hours, before the infection has a chance to become established. You have become immune to it.

If on the other hand the infection is new to your body, then it may have time to take hold before your immune system can produce enough of the antibody needed to deal with it. (This is why I spend a day bolting between bedroom and bathroom in the house in Spain where I wrote some of this book. My immune system had not previously encountered the virus which got into my insides. This virus causes no problems to the Spanish people around me, whose immune systems had got to grips with and produced antibodies against the virus soon after birth.)

T-CELLS: IMMUNITY'S SAMURAI

Antibodies are part of a complex defence system. Our bloodstreams are patrolled by, among other immune cells, a superior class called T cells. Their full name is Thymus-derived lymphocytes, because they derive some of their remarkable abilities from spending part of their youth in the thymus gland, an organ situated above the heart.

T cells have the ability to identify foreign microorganisms in the body. When the ceaselessly patrolling T cells identify such an invader, they may do one or both of two things. They may attack it themselves in a deadly hand-to-hand combat known as the cell-mediated immune response. Or they may stimulate another kind of immune cell, the so-called B cell (bone marrow derived lymphocyte), to attack the micro-organism by making antibodies against it.

B-CELLS MAKE ANTIBODIES

An antibody is a complex protein molecule, with a three-dimensional chemical structure which makes it the right shape to react with and bind fast onto just one corresponding antigen molecule, in a reaction similiar to doing a part of a jigsaw puzzle. Human B-lymphocytes are able to make something like one hundred million different antibodies, each one able to react with great specificity with just one antigen. The binding of an antibody to an antigen on the surface of a virus particle (or a bacterium, or a parasite), acts rather like the dropping of an incendiary bomb on a target. It may start the process of destruction of the target itself, but it also marks it down for other immune cells to come and attack the virus or whatever it is in a cell-mediated attack.

The enormous number of antibodies our B-cells can produce makes our defences against disease very effective. As soon as their workings were understood, scientists began to speculate on what use might be made of antibodies if they could be made outside the body, for use as drugs. But before antibodies could be used, or even tested, a way had to be found to make them outside the body. Antibodies can only be extracted from human blood in minute quantities and in very impure mixtures.

MONOCLONAL ANTIBODIES

In 1975 Dr. Caesar Milstein and Dr. George Kohler, both working at the Medical Research Council's Molecular Biology Laboratory at Cambridge, England, reported their discovery of how to make any wanted antibody outside the body for as long as the antibody might be required. The technique is simple and ingenious. Milstein and Kohler took the antigen against which an antibody was wanted and injected it into a mouse. The mouse made antibodies against the antigen. Then the mouse was anaesthetised and the cells which make antibodies were removed and grown in the laboratory

The particular cells making the wanted antibody were identified and fused with other cells, chosen simply because they grow strongly and divide fast, thus forming a culture of hybrid, fused cells, called a hybridoma. This hybridoma went on producing the antibody indefinitely. The cells also went on dividing and growing vigorously. In this way as large a cell culture as was needed could be built up to produce as much of a wanted antibody

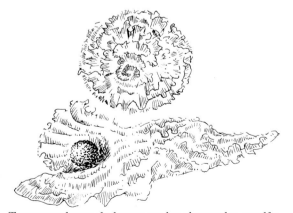

Two macrophages: the bottom one has elongated to engulf a small particle.

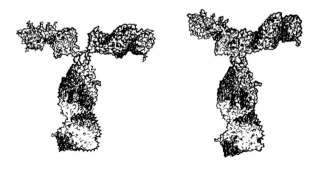

A 'T' cell joining together to attack a foreign micro-organism.

as was needed. The antibody was produced in a pure form and in relatively large quantities.

Antibodies known as monoclonal antibodies have been made in this way ever since 1975. Their production now preoccupies biotechnologists in thousands of labs all over the world. Monoclonal antibodies are used for many purposes in research. A pure such antibody can be used to identify and to locate its corresponding antigen with unerring accuracy and specificity.

Here is just one example. Earlier on we mentioned Dystrophin, the protein normally made by a gene which, when defective or absent, causes muscular dystrophy. When the scientists involved had pinpointed the gene, and made dystrophin – the protein the gene codes for – outside the body, they next made a monoclonal antibody against dystrophin. They did this by injecting dystrophin into a mouse and hybridising the mouse cells making the antibody. Then they used the antibody to locate the dystrophin which healthy genes make naturally in muscle cells. It was done by applying dabs of antibody to muscle tissue and watching for the site in the muscle where the antibody found its opposite number, its antigen, the protein dystrophin, to react with. In this way the monoclonal antibody technique was used to help track down the cause of muscular dystrophy.

Monoclonal antibodies are used widely to locate specific proteins in human and animal tissue. They have greatly speeded up the whole process of understanding how our bodies work. As well as being used for research, many scientists and doctors believe they also have great potential value in both medicine and industry. We'll look at the industrial uses in a later chapter. Suffice it to say here that antibodies used as catalysts, like natural enzymes, may prove so effective and to have so many uses that they could be largely responsible for an invasion of chemical industry by biotechnology which will help make industry safer as well as more efficient.

GUIDED MISSILES

In medicine, one use for antibodies made outside the human body has already been worked on for several years, though it is still only being used experimentally. This is to target drugs to attack cancer tumours selectively. Monoclonal antibodies against cancer cells are made and cell-killing drugs attached to the antibodies. If all goes according to plan, the antibodies will attach themselves to cancer cells but not to normal cells, and will bring the drug molecules into contact with the cancer cells to kill them.

The hope is that, by concentrating very toxic drugs onto tumours and away from normal tissue, this targeting technique will allow higher doses of more toxic drugs to be used against cancer without causing unacceptable damage to normal tissue. This should increase the chances of eliminating all cancer cells and achieving complete cures. It is a logical approach but there are considerable problems to overcome before it can be used on a large scale.

One of the drugs being tested for use in this way is ricin, a very deadly poison produced by plants. The chemistry of both the ricin molecule and that of the antibody it is attached to have to be rejigged, so that the ricin no longer enters normal cells, while the antibody is redesigned so that on attaching itself to cancer cells it somehow pulls the ricin into the cell after it. This is not proving easy to achieve.

Another problem is that no one has yet found an antigen – a protein on the surface of cancer cells – which is unique to the cancer cells and not found on any normal cells. Some antigens on cancer cells are found only on a small proportion of normal cells. But no antigen has yet been found to which toxic drugs could be targeted without any fear of simultaneously concentrating them onto some normal tissue somewhere in the body.

PREVENTING REJECTION

So using antibodies to guide drugs to their targets is still some way off. But antibodies are finding other medical uses. One that seems promising is in trying to prevent the rejection of transplanted organs.

Transplanted organs such as kidneys are recognised as foreign by the immune system of the person receiving the organ. Unless the immune reaction against the organ is suppressed, the organ will be attacked, damaged and perhaps destroyed. At present, rejection is prevented by the use of drugs such as Cyclosporin A which suppress most of the immune system. These drugs may have to be taken for life and because they affect most of the immune system, they greatly reduce the person's ability to combat disease for as long as they are taken.

An antibody evolving 'arms' to grapple with an antigen.

Surgeons in Dulwich hospital in London and scientists in the Department of Pathology in Cambridge have led the world in developing techniques to prevent rejection by the use of antibodies. One of the antigens which makes a transplanted kidney recognisable as foreign is found, not on the kidney itself, but on blood cells which are trapped inside the kidney when it is transplanted. The new approach involves making antibodies which destroy this antigen, thus greatly reducing the strength of the immune reaction against the kidney.

A team led by Professor Herman Waldman at Cambridge have made antibodies against the blood cell antigen. Kidneys to be used for transplants at the Dulwich hospital are treated with these antibodies, after the kidneys have been removed from donors and before they are implanted into patients. Surgeons at Dulwich hospital gave 77 of their transplant patients either kidneys treated with the antibodies, or untreated kidneys. All the patients were also given the usual drugs to suppress rejection. Only 18% of those given the antibody treatment showed any signs of rejection. 64% of those who weren't given the antibody showed signs of rejection.

These are only preliminary results. The doctors involved hope to see them repeated at other hospitals. But they are still so striking that those involved are prepared to say that their technique, which is simple, cheap and apparently without side effects, should be tested for other organ transplants such as heart, liver and pancreas.

Professor Waldman is now working to extend the technique to prevent rejection altogether. Kidneys are recognised as foreign by three sets of antigens, of which only one is on blood cells. The other two are on the kidney itself. Antibodies which fastened onto and destroyed the kidney antigens would damage the kidney itself, and so defeat the purpose of the transplant. Waldman's team is pursuing another approach. He is making antibodies which attack not kidney antigens, but the particular group of cells of the patient's immune system which would otherwise recognise the organ as foreign and attack it.

These antibodies are being designed to attack only the small subset of the cells of the immune system responsible for rejection, leaving all the rest of the immune system to defend the patient against disease. By combining these antibodies with those already being used against the blood cells in the kidney, Professor Waldman and his colleagues hope to develop a way of preventing rejection which only has to be used for a limited period, and leaves the patient's immune system still able to fight disease.

Helping Paralysed People to Walk

Another promising experimental use for antibodies is in trying to help people paralysed beneath the waist or neck to walk again. Dr. Martin Schwab and Dr. Lisa Schnell of the Institute of Brain Research in the University of Zürich in Switzerland have made exciting progress where all before them have failed (though using their technique to treat paralysed people is several years away).

Nerves outside the brain and spinal cord, peripheral nerves as doctors call them, grow again when they are cut. The cut doesn't heal. What happens is that the nerve on the far side of the cut dies while a new nerve grows out from the inner edge of the cut, along the track left by the dying nerve. But nerves in the spinal cord and brain don't grow again after they have been cut. A few years ago, neurologists identified nerve growth factors; substances the body produces naturally which stimulate nerve growth. Cloning techniques have been used to make these nerve growth factors outside the body, by cloning the genes for them. Nerve growth factor made like this has been used in animal experiments to try to stimulate severed spinal nerves to regenerate, but without success.

Drs Schwab and Schnell tried a different approach. They discovered that the reason spinal nerves do not regenerate is that natural substances that inhibit nerve growth are produced in the spinal cord. No amount of added nerve growth factor can overcome the inhibitory effects of these substances. Instead, the Swiss team made antibodies against the nerve growth inhibitors, and applied these antibodies to severed spinal cords in rats. The antibodies destroyed the growth inhibitors and the spinal nerves then started to regenerate. When the team last published results (in January 1990, at the time of writing) the nerves had regrown more than half the length of the rat's spinal cord.

Now the doctors are working to find a way in which the antibodies, or perhaps smaller molecules having the same effects, could be applied to severed spinal nerves in human patients. In the long term it may also be possible to use the same antibodies to treat brain diseases and injuries where regrowth of brain and not nerve cells is required. But Dr. Schwab emphasises that no human tests can be expected for six or seven years.

Attacking Leukaemia

Returning to cancer, there are ways in which antibodies on their own can be used to treat cancers, without attaching the antibodies to toxic drugs. Leukaemia is one cancer being attacked in this way. At least two teams, at the Cambridge Molecular Biology Laboratory and at the US National Institutes of Health, have used antibodies against leukaemic cells (white blood cells produced by bone marrow cells which have become cancerous and are dividing uncontrollably), to destroy the cells.

In Germany Dr. Peter Krammer of the Cancer Research Centre in Heidelberg has shown that antibodies against one class of receptors on the surfaces of cancer cells make the cancer cells destroy themselves when the antibodies react with the receptors. The antibodies have been tested on human tumours transplanted into mice, and have been shown to make the tumours shrink. This research is at an early stage and the exact mechanism isn't understood. But clearly the idea of using antibodies against receptors to send self-destruct signals to cancer cells is very attractive.

Preventing Rheumatoid Arthritis and Multiple Sclerosis

Research aimed at treating multiple sclerosis using antibodies is quite well advanced. The aim is to make antibodies against the immune cells responsible for the damage to the sheaths of nerves and inject them into patients. The idea has been tested in mice affected by a condition which closely mimics human multiple sclerosis, with promising results. But there may be more problems in using antibodies to treat human multiple sclerosis. More than one group of immune cells are involved in the harmful auto-immune reaction. Different classes may be involved at different times. This may make it very difficult to block all the harmful cells using antibodies. Nonetheless, such treatments might considerably improve the condition of patients, even if they weren't cured.

Mass-produced Antibodies

Making monoclonal antibodies in hybridomas, using Milstein and Kohler's technique, provides sufficient quantities of antibodies for research applications where tiny amounts (a few grams at most) are all that is needed. Hybridomas can also supply enough antibody for first-stage medical tests, where only a few patients are treated. But when the tests give encouraging results – as is happening now in some tests and may happen with more in the next few years – doctors will need to move on to full-scale clinical trials involving hundreds of patients. Then, if the trials go well, treatments using antibodies will need to be made widely available to many thousands of patients. In that event not grams but kilogrammes of antibodies will be required to treat all those in need.

Another problem with the hybridoma technique is that antibodies made by hybridomas are foreign to the human body. Hybridomas are made by fusing rat or mouse spleen cells producing a wanted antibody with other fast-growing cells (actually laboratory cultures of mouse or rat cancers). So the antibodies which hybridomas produce are rat or mouse proteins. Like any other rat or mouse proteins, if these are injected into humans they are recognised as foreign, attacked and destroyed.

So antibodies made by hybridomas can only be used to treat human disease for a short time before they are recognised and destroyed by the immune system of the patient being treated. After this has happened once, the antibodies will be recognised and destroyed too quickly to be much use if further attempts are made to use them in treatment.

Both these problems – the relatively small quantities of antibodies produced by hybridomas, and the foreign nature of such antibodies – are now being overcome. New techniques are making much large quantities of antibodies available, and making it possible to make human rather than animal antibodies.

"Filing" Genes in Bacteriophages

This has happened through a succession of breakthroughs on both sides of the Atlantic over the last three years. Two research teams, one led by Dr. Greg Winter in the Cambridge Laboratory for Molecular Biology, the other by Professor Richard Lerner in the Scripps Institute in La Jolla, California in the USA, have raced neck and neck. Both have found ways to bypass the laborious business of injecting antigens into rats or mice to obtain antibodies. Instead, ways have been found to store all the genes for making antibodies in a sort of living filing system. The antibody genes are stored inside viruses which infect bacteria, called bacteriophages. When a particular antibody is needed the gene for it can be picked out of the bacteriophage "file" and inserted into bacteria. They then produce the required antibody according to the gene's instructions.

Bacteria grow and reproduce much faster than animal cells. So using them to clone and express genes makes it possible to make much larger quantities of antibodies much more quickly than can be done using hybridomas. All the genes for making antibodies can be fished out of human cells and stored in bacteriophages as easily as they can be fished out of animal cells. So this technique will also make it possible to make human antibodies to treat disease instead of rat or mouse antibodies. This will get over the rejection problem. There are still some practical problems in the way of making human antibodies, but these are being overcome, and other ways of making such antibodies are also being developed.

Antibodies grown in bacteria still won't be produced in the sorts of quantities that may soon be needed, perhaps in only a few years time, to treat many millions of cancer patients. The quantities needed for that (and for some large-scale uses for antibodies in industry, which we will look at later), may however be provided in yet another way, by growing antibodies in plants.

The Green Antibody Factory

You will remember that the genetic code is universal, so that (with a little tinkering with bells

Antibodies in plants of the future 'absorbing' pollution.

and whistles) animal genes can be expressed in plants as easily as they are being expressed in bacteria and animal cells. In 1990 another team at the Research Institute of the Scripps Clinic in La Jolla, this one led by Dr. Andrew Hiatt, transplanted antibody genes into tobacco plants and showed the plants made perfect, functioning antibodies. The way is opening towards growing antibodies by the ton, as a large-scale, high-value cash crop.

The way Dr. Hiatt and his colleagues did it was ingenious. An antibody is made of two parts, known as the heavy and light chains. One gene is needed to make each chain. Andrew Hiatt inserted the gene for the light chain of an antibody into one tobacco plant and the gene for the heavy chain into another plant, and then fertilised one plant with the other's pollen. The offspring that grew from this produced complete, perfect antibodies.

In order to get the antibody genes into the plants, Dr Hiatt first had to prepare leaf cells with their cell walls removed, taken from tobacco plants. These naked cells are known as protoplasts and are used because it is easier to insert genes into them. Unlike animal cells with their soft membranes, genes can't be pushed through the hard rigid walls of plant cells. Next, the protoplasts with the added antibody genes had to be persuaded to behave like fertilised egg cells, and to grow into complete new plants. This trick can only as yet be done with a relatively few plants, including the tobacco plant. Tobacco is one of the very few major crops into which it is currently possible to insert foreign genes This is why so much genetic engineering is done with tobacco.

Even in Dr Hiatt's experiments, the tobacco plants that grew from the protoplasts with the added antibody genes produced a lot of antibody: 1.3 percent of the total amount of protein in the leaves of the plants was pure antibody. Hiatt believes it will be possible to boost the yield of antibody to over 10 percent of total leaf protein, by adding bells and whistles to the antibody genes. On that basis it should be possible, he calculates, to grow antibodies as a cash crop, extracted from plants and sold at a price of around £100 per kilogramme. That's about ten thousand times cheaper than antibodies made in hybridomas.

At present a very major obstacle to plant genetic engineering is the failure of genetic engineers to have found any reliable way to insert genes into the class of plants known as monocotyledons which include all the cereal crops: wheat, barley, maize and rice.

When a reliable way to insert genes into monocotyledons is found, it will have a colossal impact on agriculture (as we will see in chapter 12). Among the things that should become possible will be the insertion of antibody genes into cereal crops, so as to provide a second, high-value product – made, perhaps, in the stalks of cereals, which are now a waste product. Or antibodies might be made in soya beans, which naturally produce enormous quantities of proteins as natural food stores. Huge yields of antibodies might be achieved in soya by making the beans produce antibodies instead of their own natural proteins.

FIGHTING PLANT DISEASE AND POLLUTION

There are several potential uses for the vast amounts of antibodies which may be made in plants. One use would be as a way to help plants fight disease to which they have little or no natural resistance. A mouse would be made to make an antibody against a plant virus by injecting a viral antigen into the mouse. The gene for the antibody could be identified, isolated and cloned. Then the gene would be inserted into crop plants, which would, hopefully, produce antibodies to defend against the virus.

Another use for mass-produced antibodies, as we've seen, could be in anti-cancer therapy. Yet another could be in combatting pollution. Water plants which produced antibodies to react chemically with specific pollutants could be made, and grown in polluted waters. The plants would absorb the pollutant molecules out of the water and the antibodies would capture them. The plants could then be collected and burnt. The same technique might be used to harvest valuable metals from dilute solutions in waters around mine workings.

Dr Hiatt estimates it will be three or four years before antibodies grown in plants could become commercially available. This timing could coincide neatly with progress with the development of and demand for antibodies for therapeutic and other uses. Plants able to mass-produce antibodies may be ready just when the value of and market for antibodies have been firmly demonstrated.

I have mentioned two uses for antibodies outside medicine; in helping plants fight disease and in cleaning up pollution. In just the last few years it has become apparent that antibodies can be made to work like enzymes, the living body's natural catalysts. Because there are perhaps a hundred million antibodies, compared to only a few thousand enzymes, this could vastly widen the scope for the use of natural, biological catalysts in industry. A later chapter is devoted to these catalytic antibodies, – or Abzymes as they are nicknamed – and to the use of natural enzymes in industry and in cleaning up pollution. But before going on to look at the impact of biotechnology and genetic engineering in industrial areas, we need to review the fourth medical area in which genetic engineering is becoming important. We have talked about gene therapy, about the use of the body's natural defences as drugs and about the use of antibodies. The fourth big advancing area of biotechnology in medicine is the making of vaccines.

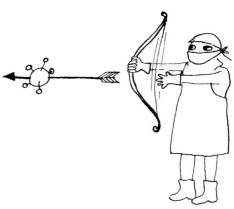

Antibody-targetted drugs.

CHAPTER 7

New Vaccines for Old Diseases

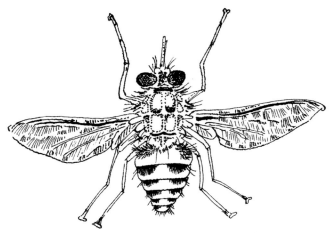

The tsetse fly, carrier of the fatal sleeping sickness.

For many years, the search for vaccines to combat tropical parasitic diseases has been largely in vain. But now, if financial support continues to be given for their development, genetically engineered vaccines may do more for human health by protecting against diseases like malaria than all the other uses for genetic engineering put together.

Tropical Parasitic Diseases: The Only Way Forward

Genetic engineering is the only way to make vaccines for most major tropical diseases. This is because the parasites that cause the diseases cannot be grown outside the body in the quantities needed to make vaccines. Conventional vaccines are made by growing viruses or bacteria in large-scale cultures, killing or attenuating (weakening) them and using the killed or weakened material in the vaccine. This is still able to stimulate a strong and lasting immune response against the virus or

bacterium, without being able to cause disease. But parasites such as the single-celled plasmodia that cause malaria, or the schistosomes that cause schistosomiasis, are so well adapted to their human hosts that they simply refuse to grow in any quantities in cultures outside the human body.

Genetic engineering offers a way to bypass this problem. First, parasite genes for antigens which stimulate human immunity strongly are identified. Next these genes are moved out of parasites and cloned in laboratory cultures, usually of E. coli bacteria. Then the bacteria make the parasite antigens. The antigens are collected, purified and used to make vaccine.

"Cocktail" Vaccines

In fact it hasn't turned out as simple as that, though in the early, heady days of genetic engineering, vaccine making did look to be quite simple. What has transpired, as our knowledge of the immune system has grown, is that one single antigen on its own isn't enough to provide complete protective immunity.

A good example of why this is the case is the malarial parasite. There are several stages in this parasite's life cycle. The first is when it enters the body from a blood-sucking mosquito, the second when it enters liver cells, the third reproduces in blood cells, and the fourth reproduces in the mosquito. Vaccines made from antigens taken from just one of these stages of the life cycle have been made and are now being tested in Africa and elsewhere. They may give some degree of protection. But there is now general agreement that a really effective vaccine will have to incorporate antigens from most if not all the stages of the cycle. The parasite exposes different antigens at different stages of its life cycle. So as to be really effective, a vaccine will need to stimulate immune reactions against all or most of them.

Another reason why more than one antigen is needed in a vaccine is that, as we saw in chapter six, the immune reaction works in more than one way. Immune cells come in two main classes, the bone-marrow-derived lymphocytes or B cells and thymus-derived lymphocytes or T cells. B cells just make antibodies. But some T-cells move into contact with the enemy and grapple it to death.

In order for the immune system to kill disease organisms infecting someone, there is usually a need for both the antibody-mediated and the T-cell mediated kind of immune response (and other arms of the immune system too, sometimes). The responses are stimulated by different antigens. So a really first class vaccine to protect against malaria, for example, not only needs antigens from different stages of the parasite's life cycle. It also needs antigens selected to stimulate different arms of the immune response.

There is yet a further refinement required of vaccines. If the antigens in a vaccine are to stimulate the immune response as strongly as a real live virus, for example, would stimulate it, then the antigens need to be presented to the immune system in a format that mimics the shape and structure of the original organisms as closely as possible. More about that later.

So in the last few years the concept of vaccines made by genetic engineering has generally been moving away from the simple idea of cloning a single gene for a single antigen in cell cultures to provide antigen material for vaccine. Experimental vaccines are now being made by cloning several genes for several antigens, chosen to stimulate both antibody – and cell-mediated immunity and

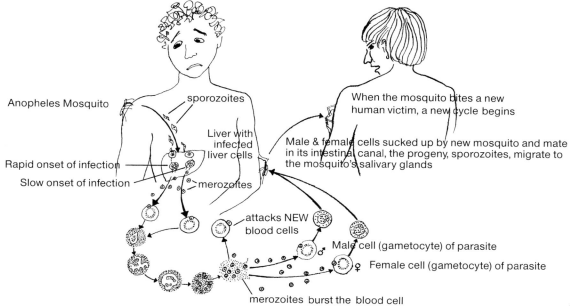

Anopheles Mosquito
sporozoites
Liver with infected liver cells
Rapid onset of infection
Slow onset of infection
merozoites
When the mosquito bites a new human victim, a new cycle begins
Male & female cells sucked up by new mosquito and mate in its intestinal canal, the progeny, sporozoites, migrate to the mosquito's salivary glands
attacks NEW blood cells
Male cell (gametocyte) of parasite
Female cell (gametocyte) of parasite
merozoites burst the blood cell

to stimulate immunity against more than one stage of the parasite's life cycle. And the antigens are being arranged in structures which mimic those of the organisms they came from, so as to stimulate immunity strongly. Making such vaccines might be called second-generation genetic engineering. As we shall see it is now well advanced, for some diseases at least.

We have seen that one reason for making vaccines by cloning genes for antigens is to get round the problem of parasites that can't be grown on a large scale outside the human body. Another reason is to make vaccines that protect against organisms which are too lethal to grow in cultures in the ordinary way. An example of this is the Human Immune Virus, HIV, that causes AIDS.

How Genetic Engineering Will Protect Against AIDS

Several different paths are being followed to make vaccines to try to protect against AIDS. Some of these vaccines are already undergoing first-stage clinical trials. Two of the AIDS vaccines under trial or development illustrate how genetic engineering can be used to make vaccines which stimulate immunity strongly, although they only contain one or two antigens from the original virus.

In the autumn of 1990 twenty healthy volunteers at high risk of AIDS were vaccinated with a vaccine which had been developed on from research by the husband-and-wife team Drs. Sue and Alan Kingsman, in the Oxford University Biochemistry Department.

"Pseudovirus" Vaccine

The concept of the vaccine grew from academic work by the Kingsmans on the genetics of yeast. This revealed that yeast cells contain particles which were nicknamed Pseudovirus particles, because they are extraordinarily like virus particles. (They may even represent an early stage in the evolution of a virus, or perhaps a degenerate virus.) Pseudovirus particles have central cores of genetic material, DNA, surrounded by symmetrical protein coats, shaped very like particles of HIV.

The Kingsmans inserted genes for HIV coat proteins into pseudovirus particles taken from yeasts. They found that the HIV proteins were then expressed on the outsides of the particles, forming parts of their coats. Then they tested the particles as potential vaccine material by injecting them into mice. They found that, because the HIV antigens were expressed on the surface of something very, very like an HIV particle, they provoked a strong protective immune reaction. But because only single antigens were present in the particles, there was absolutely no risk of causing AIDS. Nor would people working to make such a vaccine be at risk of becoming infected with HIV.

Another potential advantage of a pseudovirus vaccine is that it may be possible to use it to vaccinate to protect against several diseases simultaneously. Genes for antigens from other viruses, as well as from HIV, can be added into pseudovirus particles and are also expressed on the surfaces of the particles, which then stimulate immunity to the diseases caused by the other viruses. Being able to make such so-called multivalent vaccines is also a potential advantage of another approach to AIDS vaccine making, being developed by Professor Jeffrey Almond of the Microbiological Department of Reading University.

AIDS Plus Polio Vaccine

Professor Almond's approach is to introduce genes for HIV antigens into polio virus, which is then killed or weakened in the standard way used in making polio vaccines. Preliminary tests imply that, because the HIV antigen produced by the added gene is integrated into a complete virus, immunity to HIV is stimulated as strongly as is immunity to the polio virus itself.

Keeping HIV Out of the Body

There is a further potential advantage of this type of AIDS vaccine. It is a good example of the need to stimulate the particular parts of the immune response which are needed to attack a particular virus or micro-organism. The immune response which protects against polio requires antibodies to be produced out onto the surfaces of the mucous membranes lining the gut, to stop us catching polio from our food. The antibodies are also produced out onto other mucous membranes. So it is possible that antibodies formed in response to the stimulus of HIV antigens added into polio vaccine could prevent HIV from entering the body via the vagina or the anus. Both apertures are lined with mucous membranes.

Other AIDS vaccines won't stimulate this kind of immunity. All they can do is to stimulate an immune reaction against the virus once it is inside the body. HIV can spread from T-cell to T-cell, the cells attacked in AIDS, by making T-cells fuse together, so the virus itself is never exposed to the immune system so that it can be recognised. So there are real doubts as to whether such vaccines can stimulate a response able to prevent the virus spreading once it is in the body.

Even if a polio-based AIDS vaccine did not offer complete protection, it might be able to reduce greatly the chances of infection with HIV. From the effectiveness of ordinary polio vaccines there is evidence that the antibodies produced onto the surfaces of mucous membranes are remarkably omniscient in preventing entry by the viruses they target.

I have described AIDS vaccines first because of the appalling speed of the rate of spread of AIDS, in Africa especially. Without genetic engineering, there would be little hope of making an effective vaccine. There would certainly have been no way of discovering how HIV infects cells, so as to try to plan logical strategies to defeat it. Making new drugs to combat AIDS also depends on the understanding of infection at the molecular level. This understanding is made possible only by genetic engineering and allied techniques. AZT, the main drug used against AIDS today, works by inserting incorrect chemical sub units (bases) into the genetic code of the virus, so that its particles are wrongly assembled and cannot replicate.

Another way in which scientists hope to attack HIV uses genetic engineering differently. The virus enters the T-cells it infects through a receptor known as CD4. By cloning and expressing the gene for CD4 in cell cultures, large quantities of receptor material can be made. By injecting solutions of CD4 made in this way into AIDS patients it may be possible at least to slow up the rate of progress of their disease. Many virus particles which would otherwise have entered T-cells through CD4 receptors may instead react with the cloned receptors, which act as a kind of decoy. Tests in cell cultures have given good results.

MALARIA VACCINES: SEVERAL APPROACHES

Malaria is the most widespread of all the tropical parasitic diseases. Attempts to eliminate it by drug treatment coupled with insecticides directed against malarial mosquitoes have generally failed, because of the high risk of re-infection after treatment. Further problems are the emergence of resistance to drugs among plasmodia (malarial parasites) and of resistance to pesticides among malarial mosquitoes.

If an effective malaria vaccine can be produced which will give lifetime protection, or at least protection for a number of years, then it will release pressure on scarce medical resources and manpower. Vaccination is only one element in future strategies for the elimination of malaria. But it is, in the opinion of many experts, an essential element in such strategies. Without a vaccine malaria cannot be eliminated. And a vaccine can only be made by genetic engineering techniques.

A husband-and-wife team, Drs. Ruth and Victor Nussenzweig of New York University have been working on malaria vaccines for a long time. They have recently made and tested vaccines containing a number of different cloned malarial parasite antigens and shown that they protected mice against an infection equivalent to being bitten by fifteen malarial mosquitoes. An earlier vaccine developed by the Nussenzweigs is already being tested in humans. This is made from the sporozoite stage of the parasite's life cycle, the stage which is injected into humans by mosquitoes.

Another research team, led by Dr. Manuel Patarryo of the Institute of Immunology of Colombia's National University, has developed a vaccine containing three separate cloned antigens, all from another stage of the parasite's life cycle, the merozoite or blood stage, in which form the parasite invades and lives in human red blood cells. Tests on humans have shown this vaccine gives at least some degree of protection.

The Nussenzweigs believe the ultimate malaria vaccine, not yet made, will be the kind of 'cocktail' described earlier, containing several different antigens, all made by cloning parasite genes in cell cultures, using genes taken from several stages of the parasite's life cycle and selected to stimulate cell-mediated as well as antibody-mediated immune responses.

An even more elaborate approach, which exemplifies "second-generation" genetic engineering vaccine making, is being followed by Dr. Gerald Sadoff in the Walter Reed Army Institute of Research in Washington DC, a noted centre for work on tropical diseases. His approach, like the Kingsmans', involves displaying antigens in a life-like way. Sadoff's vaccine displays parasite genes on the surfaces of killed bacteria, typhoid bacteria and salmonellae.

ORAL VACCINE FOR TYPHOID AND MALARIA

Dr. Sadoff has inserted genes for antigens from plasmodia into salmonellae. After the killed salmonellae were fed to mice, the mice were protected against later infection with live malarial parasites. This raises the hope not only of making a malaria vaccine as an add-on to established typhoid vaccines, but also of making a malaria vaccine which can be taken orally rather than being injected. That would be an enormous advantage in tropical Africa, because it would greatly reduce the need for trained medical manpower.

Why should swallowed vaccine protect against malarial parasites which don't enter the body through the gut? What happens is that when the killed salmonellae are digested and their material absorbed, it is carried in the bloodstream to the liver. There it is absorbed by macrophages – the scavenging cells which line the blood vessels in the liver, sweeping the blood clear of debris of all kinds.

Having absorbed the salmonellae, the liver

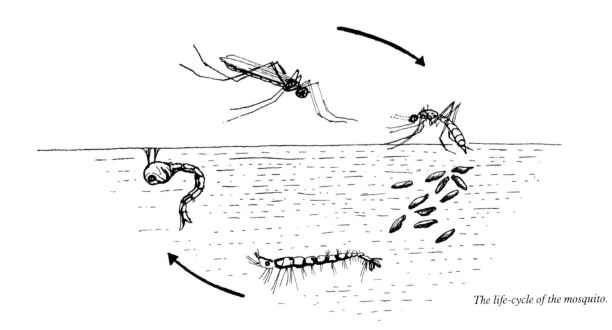

The life-cycle of the mosquito.

macrophages perform a trick which is part of their function as part of the immune system. They display the foreign antigens they have swallowed on their surfaces, so that the antigens are brought to the notice of the T-cells patrolling the bloodstream. This stimulates the T-cells to seek out and destroy any real live salmonellae they subsequently encounter in the body. Because plasmodial antigens were absorbed and are displayed along with the salmonella antigens, immunity against malaria as well as typhoid is stimulated.

So this type of vaccine, while still experimental, has three big potential advantages. One, it can be taken orally. Two, it displays single antigens on a real bacterium, so they stimulate a strong immune response. Three, it stimulates the T-cell mediated immune response, which is especially important against parasites, as well as the antibody-mediated immune response.

Very recently a research team, led by Stephen Hoffman of the U.S. Naval Medical Research Institute at Bethesda, Maryland, has made a vaccine which stimulates immunity against malarial parasites hiding in the liver, and also stimulates T-cell mediated immunity.

"ALTRUISTIC" VACCINE

Meanwhile Dr. David Haslow of the U.S. National Institute of Health, has made a vaccine which stops mice – and, hopefully people – passing on malaria. But it doesn't stop them getting it themselves; hence the name. Putting all these advances together, the effective cocktail vaccine can't now be far away.

A MULTIVALENT VACCINE

Like a pseudovirus vaccine, a vaccine made by inserting genes into salmonellae could be made into a multivalent vaccine by inserting genes for antigens from more than one disease organism into the bacteria.

A multivalent vaccine based on salmonellae could be most effective in protecting against diseases for which a cell-mediated response is especially important. Such conditions include leprosy, schistosomiasis and leishmaniasis, a parasitic disease common in Central and Latin America and the Middle East. There is now real hope of protecting against all these diseases simultaneously with one dose of a vaccine taken on a lump of sugar. But such a vaccine is some years away and it remains to be seen if it could really give complete protection against a number of diseases.

NEW USES FOR SMALLPOX VACCINE

Yet another approach to multivalent vaccines uses as its basis the oldest vaccine in the world, cowpox virus, also known as vaccinia. The term 'vaccinate' derives from vaccinia and was coined in 1798 by Dr Jenner when he first described his method of using cowpox virus to protect against the similiar, but more deadly smallpox. Until smallpox was finally eliminated several years ago the relatively harmless vaccinia was used to vaccinate against it. But in new genetically engineered vaccines which have been developed in the New York State Department of Health and elsewhere, vaccinia is now used not to protect against smallpox but as a carrier of other vaccines.

Vaccinia has a very large genome. That is, each particle of virus contains much more DNA than the average virus particle. This makes it relatively easy to add in a few more genes without distorting the particles so they can no longer infect cells. Genes from at least three viruses which cause human disease: influenza, herpes and Hepatitis B, have been inserted together into vaccinia. Tests, first in animals then in humans have shown that the immune system is stimulated by this altered vaccinia to combat these other diseases as well as cowpox.

When the live cowpox virus – unlike other vaccines it is not killed or weakened – is injected into someone, the vaccinia genes, like those of any virus, take over control of the cells they infect and make them produce more virus. The added genes are part of the vaccinia genome. So they also take over control and make the infected cells produce flu, herpes and hepatitis antigens. These antigens then stimulate the immune system of the vaccinated person to mount an immune reaction against the antigens, and the person becomes immune.

Multivalent vaccines based on vaccinia have been under development for longer than any others. Although they are only beginning to be tested in humans, elaborate and ingenious variants are already being devised. One idea is to add genes for an interleukin, interleukin 2, along with genes from bacteria or viruses. The hope is that the extra interleukin 2 produced after vaccination will stimulate the immune system to a high level of activity, at the same time as the immune system is responding to the antigens produced in response to the vaccination. In this way very high levels of protection might be achieved.

A vaccinia-based AIDS vaccine has also been tested with encouraging results. But a disadvantage may be that such vaccines won't be effective in people who have already been vaccinated against smallpox.

GENES TO MAKE PARASITES HARMLESS

A different approach to using genetic engineering to try to protect against tropical parasitic diseases comes from Professor Lex van der Ploeg, at Columbia University in New York. Instead of taking genes out of parasites and cloning them to produce individual antigens, he is *adding* genes to parasites, to make it possible to use live parasites in vaccines without risk of causing disease.

Lex van der Ploeg is the first scientist to have successfully targeted genes to precisely-known sites in the chromosomes of parasites. (Other people have done this in mice and farm animals, as we'll see in chapter eleven, but Professor van der Ploeg has been the first to do it with parasites.)

In order to survive in the human body, parasites depend crucially on certain enzymes. By targeting other genes to replace the genes for these enzymes, Professor van der Ploeg has produced genetic variants of parasites which, while able to live in the laboratory, can only survive for a short time in the human body and cannot reproduce there. His aim is to use this technique to produce harmless

versions of the parasites that cause Leishmaniasis. This is a serious, often fatal disease common in Central and Latin America and in the Middle East. The hope is that, though they will be unable to cause disease, such parasites used in vaccines will stimulate immunity as strongly as a natural infection, because they will be not only intact but alive when they entered the body.

It may also prove possible in this way to overcome another problem in making vaccines to protect against tropical diseases. This is the problem of growing parasites outside the body. By adding extra genes to the parasites, they might be enabled to feed on foodstuffs provided in the laboratory, rather than on their natural food in the human body. But that is a longer-term target.

FROM ARMADILLOS TO CLONED VACCINES

The inability to grow a disease organism on a large scale outside the body is also the problem faced by those trying to make a vaccine to protect against leprosy. For many years it was impossible even to grow enough of them to study the leprosy bacteria in the laboratory. Then scientists at Britain's National Institute for Medical Research discovered how Mycobacterium (M.) leprae, to give it its proper name, could be grown in the footpads of mice.

The research this made possible led on to the further discovery that M. leprae will grow in the bodies of nine-banded armadillos. Enough bacteria have been collected from farmed armadillos to make it possible to produce a vaccine, made from killed M. leprae, which has been under trial in Malawi in Africa and in India. Earlier trials of the armadillo vaccine in Venezuela gave encouraging results. But because leprosy develops very slowly, it will take several more years to evaluate the

The 9 banded armadillo....

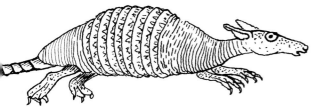

effectiveness of vaccination.

If the vaccine made from M. leprae and grown in armadillos is effective, then there will be a huge demand for vaccination to protect against leprosy. In India alone, where there are about 300,000 new cases of leprosy every year, there will be a requirement for many millions of doses of vaccine. But armadillos breed slowly and produce only limited quantities of bacteria, which are hard to extract from their bodies and to purify. Many may also question the ethics of slaughtering huge numbers of animals to produce vaccines, which is something different from using limited numbers in research which, once completed, requires no more animal sacrifice. Where will the needed quantities of leprosy vaccine come from?

Again, genetic engineering gives reason for hope. In order to protect against M. leprae, a vaccine will have to stimulate the cell-mediated arm of the immune response. Research has shown that this is what mainly attacks leprosy bacteria in the human body. Scientists in five nations – the Netherlands, the UK, Norway, Australia and the USA – have discovered how to stimulate the human body so its T-cells will be prepared to attack any M. leprae that invade it.

The international team have identified antigens on the surfaces of the leprosy bacteria which are recognised and attacked by T-cells. They did this by collecting T-cells from blood samples from people who were known to be infected with M. leprae but who had successfully resisted the infection, developing only the relatively mild, tuberculoid form of the disease rather than the serious, progressive, lepromatous form. The T-cells were tested in the lab against various different antigens from the surfaces of leprosy bacteria. In this way the scientists were able to identify two antigens which were recognised as targets and attacked by the majority of T-cells from people with resistance to leprosy. These are the antigens which, perhaps with others added, are likely to be found in a future vaccine, made by genetic engineering in the usual way, by cloning and expressing the genes for the antigens. A vaccine made in this way could bypass the problems of growing M. leprae on a large scale.

SCHISTOSOMIASIS

Schistosomes are multicelled microscopic parasites responsible for the very common tropical parasitic disease schistosomiasis, also known as bilharzia. This is a chronic debilitating disease spread by fresh-water snails where people wade barefoot in streams and ditches. Schistosome larvae from the snails invade the human liver and lodge there as parasites, causing gross swelling of the stomach and legs. Bilharzia has actually been on the increase in recent years because of major new irrigation and hydroelectric projects. Like other parasites schistosomes will not grow in culture, so genetic engineering offers the only realistic route to making a vaccine. But the

The schistosome larva, carrier of bilharzia.

How the water-bourne larvae of water-snails infect humans with bilharzia.

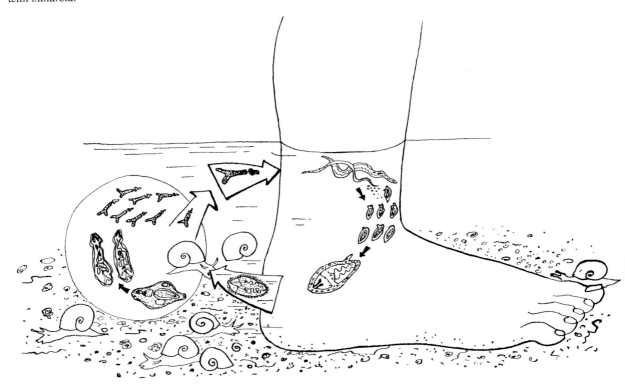

parasites are much larger than the single-celled plasmodia that cause malaria or the trypanosomes that cause leishmaniasis. The immune reaction that has to be stimulated to kill schistosomes is correspondingly more complex.

Four extra classes of cells of the immune system will have to be stimulated by a vaccine to protect against schistosomiasis, as well as the usual T-cells and B-cells. (These extra classes are macrophages which are general-purpose scavengers, oesinophils which play a special role in attacking parasites, and two other kinds of cells.) So as to be effective, a vaccine must stimulate the lot.

Professor Andrew Capron's group in Lille University in France have found a schistosome antigen which stimulates all four classes of immune cells. Professor Capron has made a vaccine containing this antigen by cloning genes from schistosome larvae. He has shown that the vaccine protects rats, hamsters and then baboons against subsequent infection with live larvae. How much protection this or other vaccines being developed will confer in humans, and for how long, remains to be seen. But a vaccine giving only partial protection against schistosomiasis would still be of enormous value, used in conjunction with drugs and molluscicides (snail-killing chemicals) in combating schistosomes.

An extra problem in making vaccines to protect against parasites is that they have often evolved highly efficient ways of evading the human immune system. The malarial parasite embarks on each successive stage of its life cycle inside the human body with a new and different set of antigens, so that an immune response against one stage is useless against another. Soon after arriving in the human body the schistosome covers itself with a layer of human protein antigens so that it is undetectable as foreign by the immune system. This is why a vaccine to protect against schistosomes has to be made from larval antigens, so that it will generate an immune response against the larva which, hopefully, will attack and destroy it before it has time to disguise itself with human antigens.

Evasive "Tryps": Intractable Sleeping Sickness

The best of all tropical parasites at evading the immune response is one of the class called trypanosomes, Trypanosoma brucei, which causes human sleeping sickness in Africa. At intervals this parasite, known as a 'tryp' for short, changes all the antigens on its surface. This means that, even if the human host's immune system mounts a successful attack on tryps living in it, while this response may annihilate the great majority of the parasites, it will have no effect on a small minority. These are the ones which have recently changed their antigen coats and so are no longer targeted by the antibodies or the T-cells of the host's immune reactions.

These few survivors will rapidly multiply into a new population of tryps. Once again they will be identified as foreign and attacked. And once again a few who have just changed their coats will survive and multiply. And so on.

It has to be admitted that all the resources and ingenuity of genetic engineers have failed to come up with anything that looks like an answer to T. brucei. There is simply no way in which a vaccine can be made to protect against a parasite that keeps changing its antigens. Instead, research is concentrating on ways to stop the trypanosome changing its coat, or at least to slow it up for long enough to give the immune system time to catch up and destroy the tryp naturally.

After many years new drugs, notably Ornidyl which has been nicknamed the "Resurrection drug" because of its dramatic effects on the most

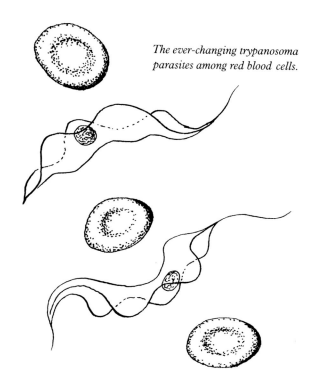

The ever-changing trypanosoma parasites among red blood cells.

advanced cases of sleeping sickness, are at last coming into use against T brucei. But a vaccine remains impossible. An anonymous immunologist paid this poetic tribute to his intractable enemy, (inspired by T S Eliot's Practical Cat McCavity).

Trypanosome, A Mystery Bug

Trypanosome's a mystery bug, and cleverer than most,
He is the master parasite that can invade the host.
The bafflement of lymphocytes, immunity's despair,
For when they reach the scene of crime, Trypanosome's not there.!
Trypanosome, Trypanosome, there's no bug like Trypanosome.
He's got a thousand aliases coded on his chromosome.
His rapid variation is dependent on a gene,
So when the cells locate him he has vanished from the scene.
They seek him in the bloodstream, they seek him in the spleen,

Tryps…repeatedly changing coat.

But in every body organ it's as if he'd never been.
Trypanosome's a wiggly bug and uniflagellate,
You can see him down the microscope, unless you look too late.
His coat is glycoprotein and a powerful antigen,
But to make a full description is beyond my feeble pen.
In appearance protozoan, but a demon of disguise,
He hides his true identity, and lives a life of lies.
They say that all the parasites of tropical disease
(I might mention the Plasmodia and such great names as these),
Are amateur infections, while Trypanosome stands firm,
The Master of avoidance, – Napoleonic Germ!

FINDING THE MONEY

I've mentioned only some of the ingenious and hopeful ways in which genetic engineering is being developed to attack the scourges of the tropics; among them malaria, schistosomiasis, leprosy and now AIDS. Genetic engineering is vitally needed by the developing world. But putting it to work isn't easy. As one scientific problem is solved, often another looms ahead. And there are the ever-present problems of money and resources. How can pharmaceutical companies be persuaded to devote the effort needed to mass-produce vaccines and drugs for use in areas that can't afford to pay for either their development or their use?

But the international agencies, most notably of course the World Health Organisation with its tropical diseases programme, are supporting many research programmes worldwide. Some drug companies have already set good examples. Marion Merrell Dow are providing a new drug, Ornidyl at the same cost as earlier drugs for the treatment of sleeping sickness, while Merck, Sharpe and Dohme are providing Ivermectin, a relatively new drug for the treatment of another parasitic disease, onchocerciasis, (river blindness) freely over large areas. A similar generous and enlightened approach to the provision of vaccines, when they have been proved efficacious, might allow vaccination to be provided on a sufficiently large scale to turn the tide against malaria and some of the other scourges of the tropics.

Genetic engineering is of unique value for making vaccines for tropical diseases. But genetic engineering is also producing important vaccines for the developed world. Perhaps the most exciting of these is a vaccine intended to protect against cervical cancer, which is being developed by Professor Bill Jarrett's team at Glasgow University.

A CANCER VACCINE

More than two thousand women die of cervical cancer every year in the UK alone. In recent years it has been shown that the disease is caused by a virus called a Papilloma virus, which is spread from woman to man to woman by unprotected sexual intercourse. After infection, other factors – such as (surprisingly but demonstrably) smoking – may be required to trigger cervical cancer. But without infection with papilloma virus it now seems very unlikely that cancer of the cervix ever develops. So a vaccine which could protect against infection with the virus could gradually eliminate the disease.

Some of the enthusiasm about Professor Jarrett's work is because cervical cancer has been on the increase, as a consequence of the increase in unprotected sexual intercourse, in turn due to oral contraceptives. Some of the enthusiasm is also due to the hope of curing as well as preventing cervical cancer through this vaccine, if the disease is caught at a sufficiently early stage.

The Papilloma virus is yet another cause of a disease organism that won't grow in laboratory cultures to provide vaccine. Once again genetic engineering has bypassed the problem. Professor Jarrett has identified the antigens which stimulate immunity and cloned and expressed the genes for them. A vaccine made from antigens made in this way hasn't yet been tested in women. But nonetheless there is already considerable optimism about the vaccine, because a very similar vaccine for a similar disease has been tested in cattle, and has been shown to work.

The cattle vaccine was tested by first infecting cattle with papilloma virus and then vaccinating them. After eight weeks the cattle developed tumours. But after twelve weeks the tumours had shrunk and then disappeared.

This suggests one way in which the human vaccine might be used. Women whose smear tests have revealed the pre-cancerous changes in cells which often lead on to cancer, and who today often have to be treated by surgery, may need to undergo surgery to remove part of or the whole of the womb. The hope is that vaccinating such women will stimulate an immune reaction which will destroy the papilloma virus infecting the cells of the neck of the womb, and so prevent them becoming cancerous. This would do away with the need for surgery altogether.

The initial cost of such a vaccine may be quite high. Like other vaccines made by genetic engineering, it will at first be more expensive than a conventional vaccine. But Professor Jarrett's team is working to identify the relatively small part of the papilloma virus antigen molecule which actually stimulates an immune reaction. When this is done, it may be possible to replace the relatively expensive business of cloning genes and expressing them to produce proteins with cheaper synthetic chemistry, used to produce just the bits of antigens that matter.

SMALLER MOLECULES: SIMPLER VACCINES

This business of identifying parts of antigens which actually stimulate immunity so they may be synthesised and used in vaccines, is important "second-generation" genetic engineering. It is being attempted for other vaccines. If such small molecules can stimulate immunity on their own without the rest of the protein antigen molecules – a big IF – then vaccines made from cheaply synthesised bits of antigens could be considerably cheaper than vaccines made from complete antigens made by gene cloning.

While such vaccines could not have been made without prior research depending upon genetic engineering, triumphant chemists (some of whom have been getting uneasy about the growing take-over of pharmaceuticals by biotechnology) are pointing out that this nonetheless marks a return to conventional chemistry for making vaccines.

It is worth pointing out that not only vaccines but other products of biotechnology – interleukins, antibodies and enzymes for example – may eventually have their large and cumbersome protein molecules replaced for clinical use by molecules perhaps one-tenth the size, composed only of the small part of the original molecule which actually performs the wanted reaction. But different amounts of different molecules may be needed for different purposes. For example, if all an antibody molecule is needed for is to react specifically with an antigen, so as to target a toxic drug to it, then only a very small bit of the antibody molecule is needed. But if the antibody is also required to do what it does in nature, and to initiate a natural chain reaction designed to kill the organism of which the antigen is part, then more bits of the antibody molecule are required.

CHAPTER 8

CANCER AND ONCOGENES

Understanding how genes work, and new techniques for identifying and examining genes, have enabled startling progress to be made in understanding the causes of cancer, especially in the last two or three years. A research area which looked horrifically complicated only ten years ago is now making exciting sense. This is coming about through using genetic engineering and PCR technology to study what have been christened Oncogenes, cancer genes – because in one way or another they can cause cancer, or help to cause cancer, when they malfunction.

About thirty oncogenes are known; by the time this is published more will probably have been found. They are all genes with important functions in normal, healthy cells. They only cause (or help to cause) cancer when something goes wrong with them. Like all other genes, oncogenes are blueprints for making proteins which are functioning parts of living cells. The proteins which oncogenes are blueprints for (code for) seem to be all or mainly of two kinds. They are either parts of the system which stimulates cells to grow and divide, or parts of the opposite system which stops or slows down growth and division.

When an oncogene is defective, or for other reasons behaves abnormally, then it will have one of two effects, depending upon which of these two classes it belongs to. If it codes for part of the system which encourages growth, then the oncogene will make the cell containing it grow and divide uncontrollably. The cell will be like a car with the accelerator pedal jammed down to the floor, regardless of the driver's efforts to control it.

If the oncogene belongs to the other class of oncogenes, which code for proteins which slow down or stop cell growth and division, then the cell will lose a vital part of those controls. Again using the analogy of a car, the cell will behave like a car in which the connection between the brake pedal and the brakes has been cut. No matter how hard the driver presses the pedal, the car won't stop.

Cancer cells/growth

normal cells

one cell gives the wrong reproductive message

It begins uncontrolled dividing

Sometimes cells drop off and travel through the body to form new colonies

GROWTH FACTORS AND RECEPTORS

Cells are stimulated to divide by chemical signals called growth factors travelling in the blood. Growth factors are produced as part of the body's coordinated growth and development. Growth factor molecules are received by receptors on cell surfaces. A growth factor molecule fits into and stimulates a receptor like a key in a lock. The signal of the growth factor molecule's arrival has to be transmitted down from the receptor on the cell surface, through the cytoplasm into the nucleus, because the genes which have to be expressed to make the cell grow and divide are in the nucleus. The message is carried down from the receptor to the genes through a chain of proteins. They pass it on by a series of chemical reactions, down towards and into the nucleus.

One kind of oncogene is a gene for a growth factor itself. If such a gene is switched on in the wrong place, at the wrong time, then growth factor will be made where it shouldn't be and cells in the area will receive a flood of inappropriate stimuli telling them to divide unceasingly. Another kind of oncogene is the gene for the receptor for a growth factor. If this gene is switched on inappropriately, then cells will have far too many receptors on their surface and so will be very over-sensitive to growth factor. This will lead to their being over-stimulated so they grow and divide inappropriately.

Those oncogenes are the same as normal, healthy genes. They have just been produced in excessive quantities, or switched on in the wrong place, or at the wrong time, or both. But some other oncogenes cause cancer when the gene is defective. Some such oncogenes are genes for proteins which represent links in the chain carrying the signal to grow and divide down from the cell surface receptors to the nucleus. A small change in such a gene can result in the protein it codes for being made slightly wrong, in a fatal way. The consequence is that the protein behaves as if it were constantly being stimulated by the signal coming down from the receptor, even when there is no growth factor molecule stimulating the receptor. The growth switch is jammed in the "on" position.

The same sort of change can affect a gene for a growth factor receptor. Some such changes are enough to make the receptor behave as though it is permanently being stimulated by a growth factor protein molecule, even when no molecule is there.

TUMOUR SUPPRESSION AND ANTI-ONCOGENES

The other class of genes involved with cancer, known as tumour suppressor genes or anti-oncogenes, make proteins which have the effect of preventing growth and division. These genes are continually expressed in cells which have become mature and differentiated and no longer divide. They act as brakes preventing division. In some cancer patients the tumour cells are found to have the bits of chromosomes containing the tumour suppressor genes missing completely, so the genes just aren't there. Without the genes, the proteins that put the brake on growth cannot be made at all. So there is no way for the cell to control its growth.

The first tumour suppressor gene to have been identified is called the Rb gene, because it is missing in children suffering from a rare eye cancer called retinoblastoma. You'll remember that two copies of every gene are found in every cell of our bodies. It appears to be the case that one copy of the Rb gene is enough to prevent a cell containing it from dividing uncontrollably and becoming malignant. In children with retinoblastoma, both copies of the gene are missing or defective in the cancer cells.

Other cancers are, it is believed, caused in the same way. For example in lung cancer, one Rb gene in one cell in the lung may be destroyed by a chance mutation. Then the other one may be lost through damage caused by smoking, for example. It may only have to happen in one cell. That one cell can grow into a tumour.

Many people are specially vulnerable to cancer because they have one of the normal pair of Rb genes missing in all their cells, for one reason or another. That means they only have to lose the other Rb gene in just one cell of their bodies for that cell to start to grow into a tumour. Some families in which breast cancer is common all have one Rb gene missing in all their cells.

SMOKING LUNACY

One thing this makes clear is that anyone in a family in which cancer seems common is even madder to smoke than other people are. For it is quite likely that he or she has only one Rb gene standing between him or her and cancer. Smoking is a good way to damage that remaining gene in one cell in the lung. It only has to happen once.

Another important tumour suppressor oncogene is called the P53 gene. Defects in this gene have been found in more cancers than any other oncogene, including over half the breast, lung, colon, bladder and, most recently, liver cancers studied. The protein coded for by P53 stops cells moving into the first stage of the cycle of events which ends in cell division. When the gene is defective, the corresponding defect in the protein prevents it from being able to act as a brake on the cell, and the cell divides over and over again without stopping.

AFLATOXIN, HEPATITIS AND CANCER

As with the Rb gene, both copies of the P53 gene have to be defective or missing for control of cell division to be lost. Exactly how this happens in each type of cancer isn't yet clear. But in liver cancer, for example, what seems to happen is that a poison which is known to cause liver cancer, aflatoxin (produced by the mould fungus, Aspergillus flavus which grows on damp crops in storage) causes one chance mutation in one P53 gene in one liver cell. This may then make the other gene vulnerable to damage or destruction by another carcinogen, hepatitis B virus. Or it may be that one gene is lost by chance and then the other is damaged by the virus or the toxin. It only has to happen to both genes in one cell to start the growth of a tumour.

Identifying oncogenes will soon make the diagnosis of cancer more reliable and sometimes allow it to be diagnosed earlier, with a better chance of a cure, by pinpointing the defective genes using PCR (see chapter 2). As the molecules produced by tumour suppressor genes (which naturally inhibit growth) are identified and synthesised, so it will become possible to develop derivatives of them as new anti-cancer drugs.

Now that the patterns of how oncogenes together with other factors cause cancer are becoming so clear, cancer research laboratories are focussing vast resources on what, for the first time ever, are clear and limited targets. New and better treatments will come from this, though not perhaps in the next few years.

Aspergillus flavus.

CHAPTER 9

THE HANDBOOK OF MAN

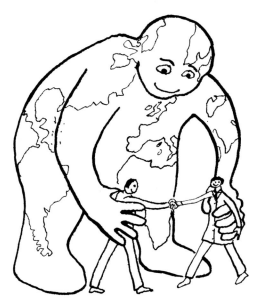

HUGO, the Human Genome Organisation.

"The Handbook of Man" is the nickname given to the Human Genome project by the Director of the Imperial Cancer Research Fund, Professor Sir Walter Bodmer. The ultimate aim of the international project is to specify the exact sequences of all the (approximately) three thousand million pairs of bases in all the DNA in a typical human cell, by around 2,000AD. About two thousand scientists are working in the project worldwide, much the largest national effort being in the United States.

Sir Walter called the human genome the Handbook of Man because it contains all the information needed to build a person. But only a tiny proportion of the human genome, any human genome, is actually made up of genes, of meaningful information. Perhaps only three or four percent.

"JUNK" DNA

If all the DNA in any human cell were to be pulled out and laid end to end, it would be about two metres long. Dotted along that length are the genes, mostly between one and two thousand base pairs long. The length is measured in pairs of bases because the DNA molecule is double, with complementary bases from each spiral joined together in pairs looking like steps in a spiral staircase. In between the genes, as you move along the double spiral, are long stretches of meaningless DNA simply known as "spacer", because that's all they seem to be for, just separating the genes from each other.

"PSEUDOGENES"

That isn't the only kind of useless DNA. Useless, that is, from the point of view of you or me. But in

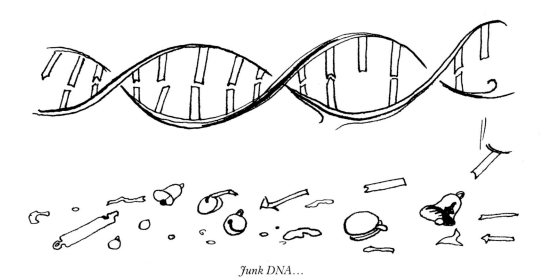

Junk DNA…

a sense DNA has a point of view of its own, which we'll come to in a moment. Dotted around between the true genes are what are called "Pseudogenes". These are sequences which, unlike spacer DNA, do contain the information needed to build proteins. But the pseudogenes have lost their bells and whistles. They no longer possess the extra sequences needed to get themselves copied into messengers and translated into proteins, so they just travel on from generation to generation without ever being expressed.

DNA's Point of View

From our human point of view, pseudogenes are useless. But evolution today is increasingly viewed from the point of view of our genes. Of course a gene – a DNA molecule – has no consciousness and no will to survive. But it is an extraordinarily effective and very tough replicator. Genes can be said to have constructed living organisms around themselves, as assorted means of aiding their survival and replication.

From DNA's point of view, the pseudogenes are doing very nicely, thank you. They have managed to dispense with their one-time contribution to the hard work of keeping the person they live in alive and kicking. They no longer make proteins. They just travel comfortably on, from generation to generation, in the protective environment created by the valiant three or four percent of our DNA – the true genes that do all the work of making the proteins that make up the body which protects all the rest of the DNA as it replicates.

Introns

Stretches of what appears to be "junk" DNA – certainly it carries no protein-making message – are scattered in the gene itself. These sequences are called Introns. When a gene is copied into messenger RNA, the introns are cut out of the messenger. What introns are for, from the human point of view, if anything, is a mystery.

Focusing on Meaningful DNA

With more than nine-tenths of it meaningless, clearly there is little point in just starting at one end of the human genome and walking doggedly to the other end, sequencing all the way. We need information about real genes and the diseases they can cause if they are defective, we need to know where these genes are and we need to sequence them. But we have little need to know the barren sequences of meaningless spacer DNA and pseudogenes.

In the next three years or so, the numerous research teams in the USA, Europe and Japan who are funded or part-funded by the Human Genome Project will sequence only about one percent of all the genes in the human body. But in the same time the scientists will have identified, and located their sites on our chromosomes, about half the total number of human genes. In about eight years time, all our genes will have been mapped. That is, we shall not only know *on* which chromosome each gene is, but also exactly whereabouts *in* the chromosome it is.

SEQUENCING BY SCANNING

Well before that, Professor Charles Cantor, Director of the Human Genome Centre at the University of California at Berkeley forecasts that it will have become possible to work out the sequences of base pairs in genes simply by scanning down the length of a gene using new kinds of enormously powerful microscopes. These are already able to reveal clearly the double spiral structure of DNA, and are just beginning to show up differences between bases. Sequencing genes by direct scanning, rather than by the present laborious chemical means, will speed up the human genome project enormously.

Charles Cantor argues for another research effort in parallel to the Human Genome Project, one directed to making it possible to work out from the sequence of bases in a gene exactly what the three-dimensional structure of the protein the gene codes for must be. It is also important to be able to work out from the protein structure exactly what the protein's function must be. The next great area for scientific funding, says Professor Cantor, is going to be learning how to work out the function of a protein from the sequence of amino acids in it, and therefore from the sequence of bases in the gene for the protein, since the sequence of amino acids depends on the sequence of bases. Without a major drive to catch up in this area, the Human Genome Project will come to an end, somewhere around 2,005AD, with 100,000 genes and the proteins they make known. But there will be precious little idea of what most of the proteins actually do in our bodies.

The Human Genome Project situation is now quite complicated. The American National Institutes of Health have set up their own Office of Human Genome Research, headed by James Watson – who with Francis Crick first discovered how DNA carries the genetic code. Their effort is concentrating upon mapping where genes are on chromosomes. Meanwhile the US Department of Energy has been pressing on with a parallel project to determine the sequence of all the bases in the human genome, developing new automated techniques to speed up sequencing to make this awesome task more realistic. So now effectively there are two human genome projects based in the USA, one concerned with gene mapping, the other with DNA sequencing.

HUGO: AVOIDING DUPLICATION

Meanwhile European geneticists were becoming increasingly concerned that these giant projects might lead to their work being duplicated, or to funds going to massive projects to sequence largely meaningless structures of DNA, rather than to specific areas where rapid and important progress is already being made in understanding key genes. This led in 1988 to the setting up of HUGO, the privately-financed international Human Genome Organisation, to try to coordinate human genome research by mutual agreement between scientists themselves.

WHO OWNS OUR GENES?

No one disputes the long-term value of mapping and sequencing genes, with all its potential for understanding, diagnosing, preventing and ultimately curing disease. But there is concern over the way in which the effort and the rewards from it are being distributed. European nations are concerned that the USA will use its financial muscle to push ahead with sequencing and will find ways to patent the applications of more and more genes vital to medicine, including those involved in conditions like cancer and heart disease, as well as those responsible for conditions like cystic fibrosis and muscular dystrophy.

United States scientists, with James Watson as their spokesman, have voiced concern that Japan may benefit hugely from US work in the human genome project, by acquiring increasing numbers of small, high-tech. US based biotechnology companies, without subscribing to the U.S. government-financed research out of which the companies grew.

Attempts are being made to avoid wasteful duplication by asking the laboratories of different nations to analyse different chromosomes. But academic scientists are unused to being restricted in this way by the demands of international collaboration. Professor Sydney Brenner of the world famous Cambridge Molecular Biology Laboratory, has already said: "We (at Cambridge) do NOT intend to be assigned part of a chromosome by some Politburo somewhere!"

Doctors in the Third World are concerned that data about genes of vital importance for the future combating of the tropical parasitic diseases, for example the genes responsible for the elements of the immune system mainly responsible for immunity to such diseases, should pass into the hands of private companies in the West. Such companies might somehow be able to patent the information and extract a high price for its use in devising new vaccines.

However, there is reason for optimism as well as disquiet. Both sequencing and mapping are needed. HUGO and the Office of Human Genome Research between them are obtaining some degree of international cooperation. And the record of some pharmaceutical companies in Africa suggests that they may be sufficiently public-spirited, and sufficiently aware of good public relations benefits, to ensure that poorer nations in the tropics are provided cheaply or even freely with the benefits that come from genetic engineering of special value to them.

Beginning to sort out the "Handbook of Man" project...

CHAPTER 10

BIOTRANSFORMATIONS ENZYMES AND ANTIBODIES IN INDUSTRY

Less than ten years ago it looked as though the main immediate uses for biotechnology were going to be in industry, and especially for cleaning up pollution. Soon, however, the medical applications of biotechnology overtook by far those in industry. Today genetic engineering is finding most of its uses either in making drugs and vaccines by gene cloning, with gene therapy just getting going too, or in agriculture. However very recent advances have led to renewed interest in biotechnology in industry. Central to this renewed interest are, on the one hand, a new awareness of the value of the extreme specificity of the reactions catalysed by enzymes, and on the other hand, the remarkable discovery that antibodies can be made to work as enzymes, widening the scope for enzyme-catalysed reactions thousands of times over.

THALIDOMIDE

Why are enzymes valuable in chemical industry? The thalidomide tragedy, in which hundreds of babies were born with crippled limbs, gives us one very good answer. The thalidomide disaster would never have happened if thalidomide had been made not by conventional chemical catalysts, but by using enzymes. The thalidomide molecule, like most biggish molecules, can exist in two forms which are mirror images of each other. One of these mirror image molecules does the job the drug was designed to do, the other caused the birth abnormalities. Conventional chemical catalysts stimulate reactions which make a mix of both forms. But there is an enzyme which makes just one form of thalidomide, the beneficial form, and not the other.

CHIRALITY: WHY "HANDEDNESS" MATTERS

The fact that when enzymes catalyse reactions they make products which are all left-or right-handed, which are *homochiral*, as chemists say, has potential economic as well as medical advantages. New medical drugs are more specific and potent in their effects on the body than earlier drugs because their reactions with their target tissues are more specific. The molecules of such drugs can very often exist in either left-or right-handed forms. Very specific reactions can only be carried out by one of the two mirror-image forms of a molecule, not by the other. So even if half the amounts of such drugs produced using ordinary catalysts are not harmful, at best they will be useless. Half the time, effort and resources that have gone into making such a drug will have been completely wasted in producing the form with the wrong "handedness", which is totally useless.

This used not to matter when drug molecules were too small and their reactions too crude and unspecific for chirality ("handedness") to be important. But it is mattering more and more now. In a few years time the waste of effort involved in making drugs that are not homochiral may be enough to bankrupt pharmaceutical companies, competing with others who are using enzymes to perform the key synthetic steps where homochiral products are essential.

ENZYMES: A NATURAL RESOURCE

Homochirality of their product is only one advantage of enzymes used in chemical industry. Enzymes are the natural catalysts which, between them, catalyse all the complex chemical reactions that go on inside living things. These reactions have to be made to "go" at the temperature of living flesh and at atmospheric pressure, unlike the metal catalysts made by chemical engineers, which often work at temperatures of thousands of degrees and pressures of many atmospheres. Over many millions of years of evolution enzymes have become amazingly efficient at catalysis. Those thousands of millions of years of evolution

represent an accumulated resource as real as coal or oil. But unlike fossil fuels, enzymes are a resource which is renewable and they are capable of further improvement, through the techniques of genetic engineering.

Growing concern for energy saving is another factor that has led to increased interest in using enzymes in chemical industry. Their use saves energy by allowing reactions to proceed at both lower temperatures and lower pressures. This has become increasingly apparent in recent years. But only the advent of genetic engineering has made it possible to begin to exploit enzymes beyond their traditional applications in baking and brewing, which do not use isolated enzymes, but whole yeast cells. Genetic engineering has made it possible to take the genes for valuable enzymes out of bacteria or fungi, to clone the genes and then either to use the enzymes produced in this way on their own, or to insert the genes for them into whatever organism is more suited for the demands of industry.

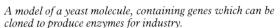

A model of a yeast molecule, containing genes which can be cloned to produce enzymes for industry.

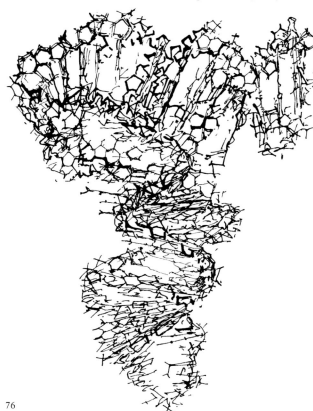

As well as the efficiency of enzymes, their ability to work in extreme conditions is proving attractive to chemical industries. One research team, led by Dr. Richard Burns in Kent University in Canterbury, is examining bacteria from the Antarctic, working on species known as psychrophiles which survive, feed and breed in temperatures far below zero. The aim is to use either these bacteria themselves, or else their cold-adapted enzymes transferred into other bacteria by genetic engineering, to clean up oil pollution in areas like Alaska where oil pipelines and wells operate in Arctic temperatures.

Another team at Kent, led by Dr. David Hardman, are going to the opposite extreme. They are collecting thermophiles, bacteria which live naturally in hot springs which are able to live and reproduce at temperatures near to – and even in one or two cases above – boiling point. Several

Psychirophiles and thermophiles.

other teams are doing similar work around the world.

One use for thermophiles being explored at Kent is in the making of cakes and chocolates. The bacteria have the enzymes needed to process fats into the forms needed for confectionery, with the advantage that the high temperatures the bacteria can work at keep the fats liquid. In this way, there will be no need for expensive and contaminating solvents. Processing at higher temperatures would also kill off any other microorganisms, and so keep the fats sterile and safe to use in food products.

That is only one of the many uses for thermophiles. But the big problem biotechnologists face in trying to get them to work is that a thermophile uses up most of its energy simply staying alive. The stresses of life at near to 100 degrees Centigrade are so great that most of the bacteria's resources are used up in combating the heat. There isn't much energy left over for chemical processing. Thermophiles have been taken from their native hot springs (they mostly come from Iceland and New Zealand) and grown in bioreactors. But while they will still work at the high temperatures demanded by processes like sweet making, they work about one hundred times more slowly than the rate required.

ANCHORING EXTRA GENES

David Hardman found a way to beat this problem. He had used genetic engineering to insert several extra copies of the genes for the vital enzymes which Bacillus stearothermophilus, to give his favourite thermophile its proper name, needs in order to perform the required reactions in the food industry. This made it work faster. But then there was another problem. Understandably enough, perhaps, bacteria object to having extra genes shoved into them by genetic engineers and very often contrive to throw the genes out at a convenient moment, such as when the bacteria divide and reproduce. But Dr. Hardman has found a way to anchor the extra genes for the vital enzyme into B. stearothermophilus, so that it cannot get rid of them.

This was done by siting the genes for the wanted enzyme next door to genes for another enzyme which the bacterium needs to digest its food. B. stearothermophilus was then faced with a tough choice. Either accept the extra genes and devote (from the bacterium's point of view but not from Dr. Hardman's), an inordinate amount of time to metabolising fats for chocolate makers. Or throw out the genes and starve, because the genes needed for digestion go with them. B. stearothermophilus knew when it was beaten and got on with the job.

RAIN FOREST RESOURCES

Bacteria which live at even higher temperatures may be found in the deep seas, and David Hardman and others hope to extend their search to the areas around volcanic vents under the oceans. Another area where the indefatigable Kent University scientists are going in search of valuable enzymes, this time led by Professor Alan Bull, is the tropical rain forests. While massive campaigns are being mounted to try to save the macroorganisms, plants and animals of the rain forests, little public interest has been shown in their microorganisms. It is harder to search for species of bacteria new to science than for previously unknown plants and animals.

But, as Professor Bull points out, it isn't necessary actually to search for bacteria. It is the diversity of the genes for novel enzymes which is wanted. DNA probes designed to seek out any wanted gene can be used to scan lots of bacteria cultured from soil samples collected in rain forests. Any genes for enzymes of interest can be picked out, cloned intensively and the enzymes tested further.

Temperatures in the middle of heaps of rotting vegetation approach the boiling point of water. Bacteria which live and work happily in such conditions are also, some of them, well adapted to working at extremes of acidity or alkalinity. These properties can all make the bacteria valuable in industry. They may, for example, be valuable in breaking down polluting chemicals in very acid or alkaline soils.

SEARCHING THE SOIL

The search is intensifying for bacteria with enzymes able to work in extreme conditions. There is no shortage of soil bacteria. Richard Burns of Kent University calculates that the quantity of bacteria and fungi beneath the placid surface of a typical one-acre field in the UK is equivalent in mass to sixty full-grown sheep. Often such bacteria need no genetic engineering to do valuable jobs. If soil samples are taken from soils which have been polluted with toxic chemicals for quite long periods, then with a bit of luck the local bacteria will already have evolved some strains able to feed on the pollutants.

From one or another bacterium's point of view, almost any molecule containing carbon is a potential food. Dr. Burns and his colleagues in the Chemistry Laboratory at Kent University, like others around the world, are putting the use of such bacteria on a commercial basis. They are offering a commercial service to industry, identifying, culturing and supplying cultures of bacteria able to clean up pollution by feeding on and so breaking down the pollutants.

A DIET OF PCBS

One way of using the natural resources of soil bacteria is to seek out strains which have evolved naturally in polluted areas. Another is to force bacteria to evolve to break down pollutants, by putting the bacteria in a position in which they have to learn to do this, or starve. This is being done with polychlorinated biphenyls, PCBs, an otherwise virtually indestructible and highly toxic group of chemicals which have been dumped all over the world in hundreds of millions of tonnes of disused electrical equipment.

Left to themselves bacteria will probably eventually evolve to break down PCBs. Different strains of bacteria are thought between them to possess all the enzymes needed. But for all the enzymes to appear together in colonies of bacteria in the areas where PCBs are dumped may take hundreds of years and Dennis Focht, Professor of Cell Microbiology in the University of California at Riverside does not believe we need to wait that long.

Focht mixed cultures of bacteria known to possess enzymes able to break down one or another part of PCB molecules and fed the mixed cultures on nothing but mixed PCBs. As the bacteria exchanged genes – bacteria do this naturally between different species – those which had acquired, by chance, all the enzymes needed to feed on PCBs found themselves with an endless food supply. The rest starved to death.

So far this project hasn't yet produced any bacteria able completely to break down PCBs. But strains able to do more and more of the reactions required are emerging. When the superbug that can live happily on PCBs does emerge, it will have a wonderful life in the wild, with a guaranteed food supply that no one else can touch at all.

GULF OIL SLICKS: A MASSIVE MEAL

At the time of writing a variant of this approach is being proposed to try to help to clean up oil slicks released into the Gulf as a result of the 1991 Gulf War, and elsewhere. Archaeus Technology, a biotechnology company which works closely with London University biotechnologists, believes there are plenty of bacteria in Gulf waters which have evolved to feed on and break down natural oil spills. Huge slicks present these marine bacteria with a huge excess of food. If they are going to reproduce fast enough to make a good contribution to clean-up, then they need other vital food elements to match the oil bonanza.

Oil-eating bugs.

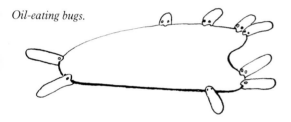

So Dr. Alex Buchan of Archaeus advocates adding nitrogen, phosphorus and various trace elements to oil slicks, in the form of ordinary agricultural fertiliser sprayed from aircraft. Fertilisers are relatively cheaply and readily available. Dr. Buchan also proposes spraying the natural detergent that marine bacteria themselves use to disperse oil so they can feed on it more easily. This natural detergent, unlike man made detergents, is harmless to marine life. It can be made by growing the bacteria in bioreactors.

Soil bacteria represent vast and still largely untapped resources. But in spite of their teeming mega billions, and their ability to evolve rapidly to learn to feed on new and extraordinarily nasty "foods", there are still only a limited number of natural enzymes available, in bacteria or anywhere else, for biotechnology to use. Bacteria evolve more by borrowing each other's enzymes than by creating new ones. An indication that adventurous

biotechnologists are already beginning to feel a shortage of natural resources is provided by the extension of their search for novel enzymes to the rain forests and Antarctica.

MAKING ENZYMES WORK BACKWARDS

One way in which the scope for enzymes is being increased which deserves a mention is by making them work backwards. Enzymes used in industry are often required to work in organic solvents, rather than in water which is their natural medium. So long as enzymes retain a minimal amount of water in their immediate vicinity, research has shown that they remain able to catalyse reactions. Dr. Peter Halling of Strathclyde University in Glasgow, who has made a special study of enzymes working in such conditions, terms them "damp" enzymes. In these damp conditions, he and others have shown that enzymes which normally depend upon abundant water for the reactions they catalyse reverse the directions of those reactions. Instead of breaking down complex compounds by reacting them with water (the process called hydrolysis), the enzymes synthesise the complex compounds with water as the other product, using as raw materials the simpler substances which would normally be the products of the reactions they catalyse.

NEW SWEETENERS

The breakdown products of normal enzyme-catalysed reactions are often cheap, readily-available materials. So being able to make enzymes work backwards opens up the prospect of making many valuable complex chemicals from cheap raw materials. Peter Halling is working with various companies to use enzymes working backwards to produce cheap substitutes for cocoa butter, new artificial sweeteners and new pharmaceutical products.

BEYOND ENZYMES – ABZYMES

What else can be done to expand the range of enzyme catalysts for use in industry? The amazing answer that has appeared in just the last five years is to use antibodies as enzymes known as Abzymes.

The body of a mammal or a human is able to make around one hundred million different antibodies. Each one can potentially be further modified by protein engineering, by tinkering with the antibody gene to produce desired changes. Genetic engineers are beginning to learn the rules of this game.

CATALYTIC ANTIBODIES

Antibodies and enzymes have a lot in common. Like that of an enzyme, the molecule of an antibody is a big protein molecule – a relatively small part of which actually takes part in reactions. Like enzymes, antibodies have evolved over millions of years to be very effective at their task. In the case of an enzyme, that task is to catalyse the conversion of a substrate – the raw material for the reaction catalysed – into a product. The enzyme actually takes part in the reaction it catalyses during the reaction, but it doesn't remain attached to its product. Once the reaction is complete, the enzyme molecule releases itself, ready to do the same thing with another substrate molecule. (All this happens quickly; a typical substrate molecule is converted to a product molecule in less than a second, and the enzyme turns to grapple with its next customer.)

HOW ENZYMES WORK

The reaction is complex and specific. The three-dimensional shape of the reactive site of the enzyme molecule fits the corresponding shape of the substrate molecule it works on like the meeting of two unusually complicated pieces of jigsaw. The pattern of electrical charges on the surface of the enzyme molecule is important as well as the actual physical shape of the molecule. I have been surprised to learn that chemists still don't know by any means everything about what happens when an enzyme reacts with its substrate. But one thing that is known is, that the reaction usually doesn't just go from substrate to product. It goes though a half-way stage, called the transition state.

The difficult part of the reaction, the part that requires all the hard work, is getting the substrate to change into the transition state. Once it has done that, it's downhill all the way. Little effort is required to make the transition state go on to make the further change into the final product of the reaction.

Imagine the enzyme molecule as a wooden piece of jigsaw and the substrate molecule as being a rubber piece of jigsaw that doesn't quite fit onto the wooden piece. Then imagine the two coming into contact and the wooden jigsaw sucking at the rubber piece till it has reshaped it enough to make it fit tight against the wooden piece. Then the wooden piece goes away and does the same job on another rubber piece.

That is a rough description of how an enzyme molecule converts a substrate molecule into a transition state molecule. The reshaping – the sucking – is done by electrical and chemical forces.

HOW ANTIBODIES WORK

An antibody reacts with its antigen as specifically as an enzyme with its substrate. The three-dimensional shape of the antibody's reactive site and the pattern of electrical charges on its surface fit the corresponding shape and pattern of the antigen with similar precision. Just as the shape of the enzyme's reactive site ensures that it will only work on one substrate, thus giving the chemical reactions in our bodies the specificity they need, so the precise fit of antibody and antigen makes possible the unerring – or at least, seldom erring – specificity with which our bodies identify and attack foreign microorganisms, without harming the body which they defend.

The difference between an antibody and an enzyme is that whereas an antibody fastens onto an antigen and stays stuck to it without changing it, an enzyme changes the substrate it reacts with into a transition state molecule and then disengages itself. I used the analogy of the wooden and rubber pieces of jigsaw to explain how the enzyme reshapes the substrate molecule into the transition state molecule. The enzyme molecule is the mirror image of the transition state molecule, not the substrate molecule. An antibody is the mirror image of an antigen. So when the two come together, the antigen isn't changed by the reaction.

MAKING ANTIBODIES INTO ENZYMES

Now suppose we select a chemical reaction in which a substance changes into something else, in the usual way, in two stages via a transition state. And then let us make an antibody, not to the original substance but to the transition state. Now suppose we mix this antibody with the original substance.

The antibody will behave like an enzyme. Think of its molecule as a piece of wooden jigsaw. That piece of jigsaw, up against the rubber jigsaw piece of the original substance, will pull it into the shape of the transition state. The transition state molecule will then change easily into the final product of the reaction. The antibody will have behaved exactly like an enzyme.

So by making antibodies to the transition states of reactions, the antibodies can be made to behave like enzymes. Since the bodies of mammals have the ability to make around a hundred million different antibodies, if only a small proportion of these can be used as catalytic antibodies also known as abzymes, they will add enormously to the potential for biotechnology in chemical industry.

THE VISION OF LINUS PAULING

Scientists first reported the successful making of catalytic antibodies in 1986, in the journal 'Science'. But the potential to try had been around ever since 1948, when the great American chemist Linus Pauling put forward his theory of how enzymes worked and wrote: "I believe that enzymes are molecules that are complementary to (mirror images of) the structures of activated complexes (transition states) of the reactions they catalyse." The making of catalytic antibodies, however, had to wait until Milstein and Kohler had provided the means to make any required antibody to order outside the body as a monoclonal antibody.

There was a further problem. Transition states last only for a minute fraction of a second and so cannot be analysed. So chemists do not know the exact structures of transition states. In order to make antibodies against them as catalysts,

Linus Pauling.

chemists have had to make an educated guess at the structure of the transition state involved, and then see if an antibody made against it actually does catalyse a reaction.

This has now been done. Catalytic antibodies have been made by first making an educated guess at the structure of the transition state of the reaction which the antibody is intended to catalyse, then synthesising a molecule having that structure and injecting it into a mouse. The mouse makes antibodies to the transition state. The cells making the antibodies are removed and made into hybrid cell cultures, hybridomas. Then the antibodies made by the hybridomas are tested to see if they work as catalysts. Some of them do.

Catalytic antibodies have now been made and tested in this way by several research teams in the USA and the UK. Sceptics said they would never be as effective as natural enzymes. Not so: the most effective are already speeding up reactions as much as natural enzymes. Enzymes speed up reactions on average about a hundred thousand times. Only the very best catalytic antibodies are working as well as that. But the fact they have got as far as they have in five years suggests that it won't be long before the performance of abzymes surpasses that of natural enzymes.

The exploitation of catalytic antibodies could have been greatly delayed if hybridomas had been the only way of making them. As we have already seen, hybridomas make antibodies relatively slowly and only in small quantities. But now that the new techniques for making antibodies described in chapter 6 are becoming available and as it is becoming possible to produce antibodies in cultures of bacteria and grow them in plants, the obstacles to the large-scale use of these artificial enzymes are being swept aside.

DISSOLVING BLOOD CLOTS

So what will catalytic antibodies be used for? The first uses will probably be in medicine. Catalytic antibodies will be able to perform reactions such as breaking chemical bonds in proteins, tasks which no natural enzymes can perform, and to carry out such reactions with very great precision. In this way it may be possible to design catalytic antibodies to dissolve blood clots or to break down disfiguring scar tissue, without side effects on neighbouring healthy tissue. Other antibodies might be designed to attack viruses. Not, like ordinary antibodies, by sticking to viral antigens and initiating destruction by other parts of the immune system, but by themselves catalysing the breakdown of the antigens, and so destroying virus particles in a new way.

A second set of applications for catalytic antibodies is likely to be in chemical industries. Like natural enzymes, but hopefully expanding the scope for them enormously, abzymes will be used to catalyse reactions where the advantages of enzyme catalysis, such as energy efficiency and homochiral products, are critically important. Where no natural enzymes exist to perform key steps in making products, especially pharmaceutical products, catalytic antibodies will be brought into being to fill the gap.

The Research Institute of the Scripps Clinic in the USA houses one of the teams responsible for developing catalytic antibodies, as well as one of the groups who have shown how to make antibodies in bacteria, and the team led by Dr. Andrew Hiatt researching antibodies in plants. These groups together may be uniquely strongly placed to exploit the market for catalytic antibodies as it develops. But those involved in the area are already prophesying that before the turn of the century every self-respecting university with a chemistry and an immunology department will be looking to commercialise its particular expertise in the making of catalytic antibodies.

BIOSENSORS

No chapter about genetic engineering in industry would be complete without a mention of biosensors. The ability to express cloned genes outside the body has, as we have seen, led to the ability to make specific antibodies and enzymes in large quantities. Because these each react specifically with just one substrate or antigen, just one other substance, both antibodies and enzymes can be used as very sensitive detectors of the presence of such chemicals. An antibody can detect a single molecule of an antigen, an enzyme a single molecule of a substrate. When the two react, the chemical reaction also involves electrical changes. These can be picked up, amplified and shown up on a meter or digital read-out, or made to sound an alarm, or do anything else required.

Biosensors like the above are much more specific and sensitive than any other kind of sensor. Uses for them are being developed in industry and medicine. Antibodies specific for various toxins and disease organisms are already widely used to diagnose disease. In the future both antibodies and enzymes will be built into inexpensive devices which will be used once and thrown away. They will enable general practitioners, and later perhaps ordinary citizens, to take over much of the work of disease diagnosis from hospital labs. Detecting pollution and explosives are other uses also being developed.

CHAPTER 11

TRANSGENIC ANIMALS

The first transgenic mouse....

In the last chapter we saw how human genes are being moved into plants so as to make the plant produce human antibodies. Plants with added foreign genes are called transgenic plants. (More about them in chapter 12.) Foreign genes are also being added to animals, for a variety of purposes: human genes, for example, are being added into mice. In this way mice can be created whose bodies in one or another way behave not like rodent but like human bodies, because they contain the human-type proteins provided by the human genes, and which still perform their human functions in mice.

Farm animals, sheep, cattle and pigs have also had human genes added to them. One aim here is to use the animals to produce valuable human-type pharmaceutical proteins, clotting factors to be used to treat haemophilia, or interleukins for example. Another reason for adding human genes to farm animals is in order to try to improve the animals themselves, to protect them against diseases with genetic resistance, for example. More

about them later in this chapter, but we'll start with mice, because of the ethical problems some feel they exemplify.

TRANSGENIC MICE

There is a breed of mice which naturally lack all resistance to disease, known as nude mice because they also lack any hair. These mice can be used, for example, to test new drugs against human cancers. If bits of human cancers are implanted into nude mice, the cancers will grow unrestrainedly because the defective immune system of the mouse is neither able to recognise and attack the cancer cells because they are cancer cells nor because they are human cells and so foreign to the mouse. Drugs can then be tested against the growing cancers in the realistic environment of a complete living body. The results give a much better idea of how the same drugs would perform in the human body than could ever be achieved through tests performed on cancer cells grown as laboratory cell cultures.

83

Transgenic mice can be used in still more elaborate experiments, in which a large part of the human immune system is transplanted into a nude mouse, which accepts it because it is unable to recognise and reject it. Various experiments are then done to discover more about how the immune system works, or to find ways of making it work more effectively to defend against disease. This involves adding genes for components of the human immune system to the mouse. Both human cancers and the parts of the human immune system that defend against cancers are now being transplanted together into nude mice, and then various interleukins are added to see if they stimulate the immune system to fight the cancer harder. If this works the proposal is to try the same experiment as a treatment for human cancer.

This ability to make a mouse behave like part of a human being is extremely valuable to researchers. It provides the ability to test out drugs,

or just to probe how things work, in the environment of a complete living body, instead of the much less natural environment of cell cultures. As more and more human genes are being transplanted into such mice, they are providing something nearer and nearer to the human body itself.

HUMANE CONCERNS

This has caused understandable concern among people who wonder how far such experiments may go. It is important to clear up possible misunderstandings here. Those who object on principle to the use of animals in research will find the use of transgenic mice no better and no worse

than any other experiments. They do not involve more suffering for the mice involved. Human genes are added to mice by injecting them into fertilised eggs, which are then replaced in the mice. They develop and are born normally, and all surgery is done under anaesthetic. The development of cancers and the testing of drugs will involve the same degree of pain and discomfort as any similar experiments involving ordinary mice, no more and no less. Either you believe mice should be sacrificed to discover how better to treat human cancer, or you do not. The use of transgenic mice does not alter the arguments.

At least, there is one way in which the argument may after all be altered – but in favour rather than against their use. An argument often used by those opposed to the use of animals in research is that they do not really simulate what happens in the human body. Transgenic mice make it possible to make the simulation much more accurately and so their use may be more strongly defended.

Another concern over the use of transgenic mice is simply due to the fact that they are transgenic. To a small but real and increasing extent they are animal-human hybrids. People may believe that monsters which are half-mouse, half-human are being created. They imagine mice with human intelligence being subjected to painful experiments.

MONSTROUS HYBRIDS?

In considering this kind of concern, it is important to realise that out of the one hundred thousand or so genes possessed by a human being, only four or five – and perhaps in the future forty or fifty – are being or will be transplanted into mice. Genes are very powerful and the effect of transplanting them is indeed to make a tiny bit of a mouse into its human equivalent. Scientists are beginning to go beyond simply adding genes to make mice produce parts of the human immune system. They are beginning to add enough human genes to make mice produce functioning parts of organs, the specialised cells of the pancreas or kidney for example. But none of this is leading towards creating creatures which are half mouse half man in the senses which people loathe and fear: which is a human brain in a monstrous part-mouse body, or a human body with a mouse's brain.

The many who deeply distrust science and scientists will say, but how do we know this is where they will stop? Once "They" know how to put human genes into mice, how long will it be before "They" do it to produce monsters? The scientists may not want to but what if some evil government makes them do it at gun point? (I know people ask this question because it has been put to me, repeatedly, ever since I started writing and broadcasting about biotechnology.)

THE ONLY WAY AHEAD

Certainly there is no body of people called scientists who are constantly creating or being driven to do things which are not only cruel and horrible but also quite pointless. Every experiment involving transgenic mice I have ever read about has as its aim the increase of knowledge which, quite clearly and unarguably, will provide the best chance of giving doctors a better chance of curing one or another disease.

Some of the experiments have this as a direct target, for example a new drug is actually being tested. In others, it is less direct. For example the aim may be to discover how part of the immune system works, so as to find better ways of stimulating it to fight disease, or perhaps to switch off auto-immune reactions causing multiple sclerosis or arthritis. Transgenic mice offer new and better ways of doing these things. As with all research – as in all human endeavour – many of the experiments will lead nowhere, because of things which cannot be foreseen until the experiments have been performed. But each experiment is devised with the intention of bringing about an increase in knowledge of a kind which is best calculated to improve the treatment of disease. They are not pointless. If one accepts that experiments on animals are acceptable if they may produce real medical benefits for sufferers from serious diseases, then one should be able to accept work using transgenic mice.

ANIMAL FACTORIES

There is, however, a real distinction between the use of animals in research, where genetic engineering may offer approaches which are both more effective and, because more rapid progress is possible, also more humane, and the use of animals as chemical production facilities. In experiments (though not in routine screening tests), animals are used in minimal numbers. The hope is always that once an experiment is over, that chapter will be closed. No more animals will need to be sacrificed and something worthwhile will have been achieved.

But the use of mice in, for example the making of monoclonal antibodies is different. Monoclonal antibodies may be needed for the foreseeable future, in large amounts. Is it right to go on using living, sentient creatures indefinitely as production facilities? It is a fact that some biologists working in this area I have met have been very enthusiastic about the development of new techniques for making antibodies using plants and in bacteria (described in chapter six), because of the opportunity for ending the routine use of rodents to make antibodies which these techniques present.

My own belief is that over the next fifty to one hundred years genetic engineering will increasingly give the human race new and extraordinary powers, and that among the problems that will come with these powers will be what to do with our power, if we wish, to transform the animal kingdom. We do not have to acquire these powers. But not to do so means effectively abandoning biological and medical research. As I hope is clear from this book so far, the next big steps forward in medical drugs, vaccines and treatments based on gene therapy, are mostly coming from the area of genetic engineering. There are no alternatives. This is where progress will come or, in most areas of medicine, it won't come at all. And not only in medicine. Real advances in agriculture, and in some chemical industries, also depend crucially on biotechnology.

Genetic engineering has acquired such a bad public image in some countries that progress in some research areas is being and will be slowed up. But not, I think, for very long. As soon as some of the real benefits begin to show their effects, the public image will change and research will speed up again. Then those nations which have kept abreast of developments will find their investment in research paying off, in new and better medical drugs, in improved crops and in some chemical industries. Those who have slowed up or abandoned research will either have to invest phenomenally to try to catch up or abandon huge areas – for genetic engineering is increasingly all-pervading – to their international competitors, and be the poorer for it.

TRANSGENIC SHEEP AND COWS

There has been also been concern about the creation of transgenic farm animals: pigs, sheep and cows. Dr. John Clark and his colleagues in the Edinburgh Institute of Animal Physiology have already inserted human genes for two valuable human substances into sheep. These are Factor IX, which is essential for blood clotting and is deficient in some haemophiliacs, and antitrypsin which is badly wanted as a treatment for a serious lung disease, emphysema. Dr. Clark has shown that the genes function and that by adding the proper bells and whistles he can make sheep produce Factor IX and antitrypsin in their milk. These substances can be extracted from milk and in a few years, after appropriate safety tests, it is hoped it can be used to treat haemophilia and emphysema.

Is it ethical to use animals in this way? Activists who attacked John Clark's laboratory thought not. If you are opposed to the use of animals for any human purpose then you will be equally opposed to their use for making pharmaceuticals. However, if you have no objection to the keeping of cows, in humane conditions, to provide milk and cheese then I can see no reason why you should object to their use to provide pharmaceutical drugs. I say cows because, although the first work has been done on sheep because they are smaller and cheaper to work with, the long-term aim is to use cows.

CONTROVERSY OVER BST FOR CATTLE

Inserting genes into embryos to create new transgenic breeds of farm animals is not the only way in which genetic engineering can be used for the benefit of agriculture. Another approach is to use the powerful growth promoters that can be made by cloning the genes responsible for them outside the body, as stimulants for growth. Bovine Growth Hormone, orsomatotrophin, also known as BST, is the best-known and at present most controversial example of this.

BST has been extensively tested in cattle, sheep and goats, given as an injection. It has been shown to increase milk yields by 15 to 25 percent, with no significant adverse effects on the health of the animals or the quality of the milk. The need for frequent injections can be prevented by giving BST in harmless implants which release it gradually into the bloodstream. The effects are reversible.

Implants of BST have advantages over other ways of increasing milk production, and even over the creation of herds of transgenic cattle. BST has an instant effect and allows diary farmers to adjust their milk production to meet rapidly varying short-term market requirements. But reactions to BST have generally been lukewarm and unfavourable, because of concern that milk is already over-produced in the West, and that the use of BST will widen the gap between those farmers able to afford it and those unable to do so. Many small producers might be forced out of business. Nations with larger dairy units, such as the UK, Netherlands and Denmark would benefit while those with smaller units, such as Greece, Italy and Germany might suffer.

GETTING MORE OUT OF GRAZING

A different and less controversial idea is to use genetic engineering to try to improve the efficiency with which ruminants (cattle, sheep and goats) digest cellulose, the fibrous substance which makes up the cell walls of plant cells. Cellulose is broken down by bacteria living in the guts of ruminants, but a significant proportion of it remains undigested, representing a wasted food resource. Scientists at the Institute of Animal Physiology and Genetic Research at Babraham near Cambridge, England, have succeeded in inserting genes for extra enzymes, cellulases, which break down cellulose into the bacteria which live in ruminants.

GRAZING PIGS

This work is at an early stage. But some genetic engineers are already looking beyond it. One idea is to insert genes for cellulases into the digestive enzgme secreting cells of the pancreas of pigs. The cellulase would then be produced along with the pancreatic digestive enzymes, and under the same controls. That would ensure that the cellulase, like the digestive enzymes, would only be produced when there was food available for it to work on. In this way pigs might be converted into creatures able to thrive on a wider variety of diets, without the need for colonies of bacteria in their guts, which, unlike the elaborate extra stomachs of ruminants, are not designed to contain them.

Other transgenic creatures are being created. Genes may be added to make a cow's milk better for cheese making. Cheese requires a protein called casein, so cows may be given extra casein genes (with bells and whistles to make sure the genes are expressed in the udder). Or milk with a higher calcium content may be produced, or milk with a lower saturated fat content, so cows could produce ready-skimmed milk. The adding of such genes to a cow will not alter the cow's appearance, its physique, or mental or physical life one jot.

Growth hormone genes have been implanted into pigs to make them grow faster and produce leaner meat, and to reach marketable size quicker and while their meat is tender. The first pigs with added genes suffered from arthritis and were infertile. More recent experiments have used the pig's own growth hormone instead of the human growth hormone used at first, with better results. Still more recently, a way to produce leaner pork by injecting antibodies which destroy fat cells has been developed.

Better for us, you may say, but what about the pig? Well if you are a vegetarian, or just someone who refuses to eat pork because of the way in which pigs are bred in modern farms, this leaves you more or less where you were. The added genes or antibodies will not alter the pig's way of life much if at all. If you accept pig farming as it is, then the added genes may provide you with cheaper and more tender pork, If you are a pig farmer, they may provide higher income.

In recent years the technical innovations available to the livestock industry have grown to formidable numbers. These now include artificial insemination, drugs to cause superovulation (the production of numerous eggs), the reclamation of egg cells from slaughterhouses for growth in culture before implantation into foster mothers, embryo sexing, cloning to produce larger numbers of identical individuals of good pedigree by embryo manipulation, long-term storage of sperm, eggs or pre-embryos in deep freeze, genetic engineering of embryos to create new transgenic breeds, and the treatment of livestock by drugs manufactured by gene cloning, such as BST.

Genetic engineering represents only a part of this movement towards the improvement of quality by biotechnology. As such it must also play a part in the pressures which make farm animals lead increasingly unnatural lives. Genetic engineering is itself neutral in terms of animal welfare. It can be used to improve the lives of animals, by increasing disease resistance, for example. Rather than calling for the abandonment of genetic engineering those concerned for animal welfare may consider informing themselves fully of the many uses to which it can be put, and then making their voices heard to press for the most humane applications.

WHY USE ANIMALS?

Those who oppose the creation of transgenic animals to produce products like Factor IX may argue that cell cultures can and do produce the same substances when human genes are inserted into them. So why use animals? One answer is economic. It may be cheaper and simpler to use animals, which don't need to be kept in bioreactors in labs. but can feed on grass in fields. Once the genes for the wanted human substances have been inserted into the pre-embryo of a cow, and that pre-embryo has grown into a cow and produced calves, the gene is there for all future generations.

No more laboratory work is needed. The production of valuable human substances to use as drugs could be combined with that of milk, by herds of transgenic cows who would live the life of any dairy cows – except, presumably, that being that much more valuable, they would be looked after that much more carefully. But it is true that their lives might become increasingly unnatural.

GOLDEN EGGS?

Amgen, a private genetic engineering company in California, produced the world's first healthy transgenic chicken in 1989 and showed that the added genes were handed on to successive generations. The genes were added to new laid eggs by the familiar technique of inserting the genes into viruses which were first rendered harmless, and were then allowed to infect the eggs.

Amgen now hope to create three kinds of transgenic chickens. The first will be made resistant to killer viruses, which spread fast in broiler houses. The second will have added growth hormone genes to make them grow more quickly. The third generation of transgenic chickens, if all goes to plan, will produce valuable human substances for use as medical drugs. They will compete with the transgenic cows described earlier. The chickens will produce drugs neatly packaged in their eggs. This will be made possible by replacing the gene for the egg white protein albumen, made in huge amounts in eggs, with the gene for the wanted substance. Ten chickens with added genes could produce one gram of, say, an interleukin every day, a lot by cell culture standards.

You may or may not object to keeping chickens in broiler houses, but adding genes to the chickens will not make their lives whether in or out of the houses, any better or worse. If chickens produce high value products in their eggs then they may be looked after better. On the other hand that cossetting might mean even less natural lives. But it won't make much difference either way. If one is concerned for chickens, campaigning should be aimed against factory farming, not genetic engineering.

FOUR-LEGGED BIRDS?

It has been suggested that genetic engineers might go further. As their knowledge of how growth is controlled grows, they might produce chickens with no wings, or two pairs of legs, because drumsticks are meatier than wings. Or chickens without feathers, to get rid of the nuisance of removing them. Amgen emphatically deny any intention of doing any such thing, and not only because they think it would be wrong. There would be no money in it because a revolted public would quite naturally refuse to buy the chickens.

YOUR CHOICE

But again, the choice, this time most emphatically, is yours. The food industry is exceptionally sensitive to the views of consumers. If, having absorbed what genetic engineering can do, you vote with your wallet for, say, free-range chickens producing valuable pharmaceuticals as well as or instead of edible eggs, then that is what you will get. If you are prepared to settle for featherless chickens to take a few pence off their price you might get them (but I doubt if the

An adult mosquito on human skin.

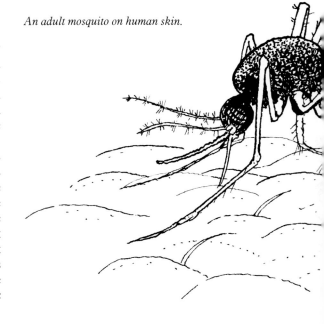

necessary legislation would ever get passed). The important thing is to understand the possibilities in order to make the informed choice.

TRANSGENIC MOSQUITOES

Mice and farm animals are not the only transgenic animals being created. Transgenic insects are also being made, and for yet another purpose: disease control. The first transgenic mosquitoes were made a few years ago in the Liverpool School of Tropical Medicine by Dr. Julian Crampton's group. The genes are injected in solution into mosquito embryos that are two hours old, using a very fine pipette. At that early stage of development the nuclei of the embryos are not separated by cell walls: the embryo is a mass of tissue with many nuclei, called a syncytium. The absence of cell walls makes it easier for the nuclei to absorb the added genes. In about ten percent of the injected embryos, the genes find their way into the cells which, as the embryo grows into a mosquito, form the reproductive organs. This means the genes are passed on to future generations of mosquitoes.

STERILE MALES

Why add genes to mosquitoes? The intention is to release them so that they interbreed with wild mosquitoes and create populations that cannot spread disease. The aim is to attempt a much more sophisticated version of a control technique known as the "sterile male" method of pest control. This technique, first developed nearly thirty years ago, involves breeding a batch of harmful insects in the laboratory, subjecting them to high doses of radiation and then releasing the insects in the wild. The idea is that the male insects which have been released will mate with wild females, but the mating will be sterile, because the radiation has made it impossible for the males to produce fertile sperm. Since many insects only mate once, or only a very few times, this steadily reduces the population of insects, as the numbers of fertile matings are reduced.

The idea has the merit of avoiding the use of pesticides. It is completely species specific, which is why a lot of work has been done on the sterile male technique, in spite of its disadvantages. Among these are the fact that male insects subjected to near-lethal doses of radiation are unlikely to compete effectively for mates in the world, outside the laboratory, and that the release of irradiated insects has to be repeated over and over again to keep on reducing the population.

ATTACKING MALARIA

The new ability to insert genes into mosquitoes has allowed research teams to envisage and then to begin to develop much more sophisticated variants on the sterile male technique. The malarial mosquito is a first target. But the aim now is not to eliminate a population of mosquitoes, as all that will do is to leave an area invitingly empty of mosquitoes, waiting to be colonised by other mosquitoes from surrounding areas.

A more subtle aim is to create a population of mosquitoes which will survive, and indeed compete effectively with others in the area, and go on taking blood meals off humans. But they will not be able to spread malaria.

Julian Crampton's team is working with genes

that occur naturally, and which make the mosquitoes possessing them naturally resistant to the parasite that causes malaria, so that it cannot survive in their bodies for long enough to be passed on to humans. One such gene makes mosquitoes produce lectins – sticky substances which stick to parasites clustered on the outer wall of the mosquito's gut and bathed in the blood which fills the body cavity around the gut. This is where the parasites normally divide to form sporozoites, the name for the stage of the parasites' life cycle which is injected into humans when a mosquito sucks our blood.

The lectins stuck to parasites act as markers for haemocytes, the killer cells of the mosquito's immune system. These do the same sort of job as human T-cells, attacking and destroying the

SPREADING GENES THROUGH THE POPULATION

The first approach may be preferable, because the resistant mosquitoes created by it will tend to be superior rather than inferior to the wild population. Their resistance to malaria may give them some advantage. If this approach to the control of malaria is to work at its best, then the genes which prevent transmission of malaria must be spread through the population as fast as possible by interbreeding, so that whole districts, and perhaps eventually whole continents, become populated exclusively by mosquitoes that cannot spread malaria. If making mosquitoes resistant to malaria is not enough to give them a competitive advantage in mating and surviving in the wild, then it may be necessary to build in other extra genes to create a sort of supermosquito.

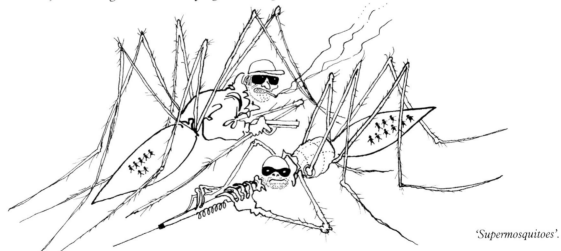

'Supermosquitoes'.

parasites. Sporozoites are never formed and so the mosquito is unable to infect humans.

There are other genes which may be used to make mosquitoes unable to transmit malaria. Two approaches may be followed in using them. One, like that described above, is to produce an insect so resistant to malarial parasites that it loses its ability to transmit them on to humans. The other, opposite approach is to find genes which would make mosquitoes so vulnerable to malaria that they would be killed by the parasites before they had the chance to transmit them on to humans.

EXTRAORDINARY PRECAUTIONS

Julian Crampton is the first to emphasise that no such creature should be released without extraordinary precautions. It would be essential to couple the genes that make the lab-bred mosquito a super-insect to those genes which make it unable to transmit malaria, in a way which would make it impossible for the two genes to become separated. If they did separate then there would be the nasty prospect of an emerging race of man-made super mosquitoes still able to transmit malaria.

Here is an example of genetic engineering

where the potential for good is enormous – the same approach might be used to prevent other insect-transmitted diseases – but where the need for the most stringent precautions is very clear.

Borrowing Insect Immunity

There is another good reason for studying the resistance of insects to human diseases they transmit. This is the hope of using the insect's defences to protect ourselves. Insects transmit many human diseases to which they themselves remain immune. Research has begun to show that they protect themselves against these diseases, as in the case of malaria, by systems analogous to but different from our human immune system. Some forms of the blackfly (Simulium damnosum) that transmit the parasite causing river blindness (onchocerciasis) are naturally resistant to the parasite. At the Liverpool School for Tropical Medicine, Dr. Peter Ham has discovered that these varieties produce substances – lectins and another group of chemicals, cecropins – which kill parasites within minutes. They seem to act like even more lethal antibodies, but their molecules are much smaller.

As with malarial mosquitoes, there is now the hope of spreading the genes for resistance into wild populations of Simulia, so as to make them unable to transmit onchocerciasis. There is also the hope of using lectins and cecropins, (or, what is more likely, derivatives of them) as new drugs to treat human disease. Insects are the most successful group in the animal kingdom, arguably more successful than humans. We may have much to learn from the ways in which they fight disease. A big first step in that direction, now being taken at Liverpool and elsewhere, is to clone the genes for lectins and cecropins so as to make these substances and discover more about how they kill parasites.

Supercats? Supersheep?

None of the transgenic animals described here or made to date are really much different from ordinary animals (with perhaps the exception of mice with whole sections of the human immune system transplanted into them). At present we do not know how to do much more than make farm animals produce human substances or grow faster, or mosquitoes resistant to malaria. But unless scientists simply abandon work on genetic engineering – which means abandoning what everyone in the business sees as the only real way forward towards most new and better drugs and vaccines – then over the next fifty years or so we are going to acquire the ability to reshape animal life much more profoundly by adding specific genes.

'Superpet'.

We will probably, for example, be able to produce super-intelligent cats and dogs. But what will they think about being our pets?

Brainless Beef

Certainly we should be able to produce animal cell cultures with the flavour and texture of beef, pork and lamb and so put an end to the slaughter of animals for food. Widespread abhorrence of the slaughterhouse will encourage the development of cell cultures to replace the slaughter of livestock. Not just steak but all the organs of animals will be duplicated in culture: liver, kidneys, heart, tripe – everything I suppose but the brain. I for one, can live without eating that.

This might mean the end of cattle, sheep and pigs, for who would keep farm animals if not for profit? Is it better to have lived as a humanely-treated farm animal or never to have lived at all? That is a question that could perhaps only be answered by a super-intelligent pig or sheep.

CHAPTER 12

TRANSGENIC PLANTS

Conventional plant breeding is a long and laborious business. A plant breeder wanting to add resistance to a virus disease, say, to other attractive qualities of a crop plant first has to search for a wild variety of the same plant having the wanted resistance. Then he has to cross this wild variety with the crop in need of improvement. The offspring, however, carries not only the gene for the wanted virus resistance but also many of the other genes of the wild variety, some of them not just unwanted but positively disadvantageous. Breeding for several more generations, with a bit of luck, gets rid of at least some of the less advantageous genes. Of course none of this is possible at all if the wanted resistance just doesn't happen to exist in the species to which the plant in need of improvement belonged.

GENES FROM ANYWHERE

Contrast this with what genetic engineering will make possible. (I say will, because for most important crops the trick still can't be done.) A wanted gene can be searched for anywhere in the whole plant kingdom, or in fungi or bacteria – or even in the animal kingdom. Once found, the wanted gene can be inserted into the crop plant in need of it in a single operation, without any other unwanted genes. Clearly, genetic engineering has the potential both to widen the scope for plant breeders enormously and considerably to speed up their operations.

What the effects of this will be will depend, as usual, upon an informed public pushing things the way they want them to go. But there is no doubt that the effects will be substantial. A well-researched study published in 1984, "*The New Plant Genetics*", predicted major genetic improvements by the use of genetic engineering to all the world's 28 major crops, before the year 2,000.

The study was produced by William Teweles of Milwaukee in Wisconsin, a consultant specialising

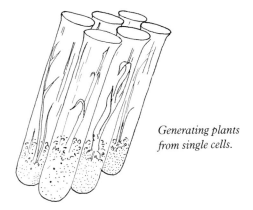

Generating plants from single cells.

in seed and plant science. He predicted that by 2,000 AD or shortly after, many crops would produce higher yields, resist pests and diseases against which their species had no natural resistance, grow in adverse weather conditions, require little or no fertiliser through being able to fix their own nitrogen, and be more nutritious. The value added to crops through genetic engineering each year after 2,000 AD, said the report, would be twenty thousand million dollars.

HERBICIDE RESISTANCE: HOW BENEFICIAL?

One of the first uses to which genetic engineering has been put in crop breeding is one which is unpopular with environmentalists and is seen by most as a mixed blessing. This is the creation of crops which are resistant to herbicides. Three different genes which make various weeds resistant to herbicides in three different ways have been identified. Chemical companies who manufacture herbicides have been quick to see the advantage of inserting such genes into crops to make them resistant only to their own herbicide product.

Like it or not, the way in which genetic engineering has been used to produce herbicide-resistant crops illustrates strikingly how fast the technology can steam ahead when there is money behind it and the promise of more to be made ahead of it. One of the genes for herbicide resistance works by making the plant possessing it produce more of the substance vital to the plant which is destroyed by the herbicide. Another gene works by changing the same substance so the herbicide can no longer react with it and destroy it. The third gene works by making those plants possessing it able to detoxify a herbicide, and so rendering it harmless.

THE ROAD BLOCK

All these genes are now available to genetic engineers to try to insert into crops. Whether or not the crops belong to the same species as the weed with the wanted gene no longer matters. But here we come to the biggest road block in biotechnology. Progress has already been held up for years longer than anyone in the business anticipated.

The plant kingdom is divided into two great groups, monocotyledons and dicotyledons. (So-called because monocotyledons produce one leaf when the seed first germinates while dicotyledons produce two.) Nearly all important crop plants are monocotyledons. But so far, genetic engineers have only been able to insert new genes reliably into dicotyledons.

IMPROVING TOBACCO

There is no doubt among scientists involved that within a few years, maybe by the time this book is published, a reliable way to get genes into monocotyledons will be found. But meanwhile most of the new ideas for improving crops by genetic engineering are being tested out in one of the few major crop plants that happens to be a dicotyledon, the tobacco plant. It's unfortunate for the public image of genetic engineering that so many of its first applications in agriculture are in a crop that many would like to see banned because of the harm it does to health. And tobacco is being made resistant to herbicides, so as to perpetuate and even increase the use of polluting chemicals – something it has been devoutly hoped genetic engineering would reduce rather than increase. It is not surprising that there is at present some doubt and cynicism about the use of genetic engineering in agriculture.

ADVANCED GENETIC ENGINEERING

Resistance to pesticides was built into tobacco in an ingenious way. First soil bacteria were scanned in search of strains which might have evolved the means to protect themselves against poisonous chemicals seeping into the soil. Because bacteria reproduce much more quickly than plants, they were more likely to have evolved the wanted resistance. A bacterium able to detoxify a herbicide, Bromoxynil, was found. The gene for the detoxifying enzyme was identified, cloned and inserted into another bacterium, Agrobacterium tumefaciens. Agrobacterium is used by genetic engineers as a natural way to get genes into plants because the bacterium naturally inserts its own genes into them, so extra genes added to it can be inserted along with Agrobacterium's own.

Normally Agrobacterium causes tumour-like growths known as crown galls on trees – hence its name tumefaciens. For genetic engineering purposes the bacterium had some of its own genes deleted, to render it harmless but still able to insert genes into plants.

A piece of tissue was cut out of the leaf of a tobacco plant and infected with the Agrobacterium with the added gene. Then the infected leaf cells were grown, with stimulating chemicals added, to make individual cells grow into complete new tobacco plants – behaving, in fact, as if the cells were ova fertilised with pollen. The new plants were tested with bromoxynil to see if they were resistant. The Californian genetic engineering company which did the work, Calgene, found that the plants were completely unaffected by eight times the highest concentration of bromoxynil that had ever been used by farmers.

Crops made resistant to herbicides in this and other ways will be profitable for those who sell their seed, and for the farmers who grow them. But they will do nothing to further the declared aim of companies like Monsanto, as well as academic scientists involved in genetic engineering, which is to reduce the use of chemicals in agriculture. They are more likely to increase the use of herbicides. Yet a spokesman for another company, ICI Seeds, one of the world's leading seed producers, has reiterated recently that one benefit from biotechnology will be a decrease in the use of chemicals in agriculture. Is this a realistic target?

Engineering Monocotyledons

There are several potentially economically attractive ways to add genes to plants to reduce the use of chemicals, and I will describe some of them. But clearly the first need is to find a way to get genes into the group to which most of the world's crops belong, the monocotyledons. Naturally a lot of work is being devoted to this by private companies, but it is still being kept under wraps. While a reliable means of inserting genes remains at the time of writing tantalisingly out of reach, the Max Planck Institute at Heidelberg has gone a long way towards it.

Injecting Genes

Their experimental technique involves injecting solutions of genes into tiny shoots on maize plants, the shoots which later form flowers. Pollen from some of the flowers which grew from shoots injected with DNA was then used to fertilise ova on other flowers grown from shoots which had been injected.

Just two or three out of thousands of seeds and the plants that grew from them from such matings were found to have incorporated the new genes when the work was first reported. But no doubt, by now, the scientists (or others in seed companies picking up the technique and developing it themselves) have achieved a much higher success rate.

Geminivirus: Another Way To Get Genes Into Plants?

At Imperial College, London, Professor Ken Buck and his colleagues have been pursuing a different route to the same end. They are developing the use of viruses called geminiviruses, which infect most cereal crops, as a way of getting genes into such crops. The Imperial College team have engineered a geminivirus to render it harmless but still able to carry genes into crops. The idea is to insert the wanted genes into a virus and then infect a field of a cereal crop with it. The virus would carry its own and the added genes into many plants and infect their reproductive organs. Later, seed derived from the fusion of pollen and ova containing the added genes would be collected and used to produced new transgenic breeding cereals.

Will it work? Professor Buck has shown that added genes get into the maize plants he has been working on. At that time he was only inserting marker genes to see if the idea worked. The next step is to insert useful genes, for resistance to disease perhaps, to see if they too are acquired by the maize plants.

The genetic engineering of the geminivirus required to make sure it cannot cause disease leaves it still able to replicate inside the plant, but now unable to infect the plant in the first place. To get round this problem, the virus is first inserted by genetic engineering, into Agrobacterium tumefaciens. This handy bacterium is then used to infect the plant and thus to insert the virus, with the added gene, along with Agrobacterium's own genes into the maize plants.

Those two examples from several projects working to insert genes into monocotyledons suggest that reliable genetic engineering of the world's major crops: wheat, maize, barley, rice and so on, cannot be far away.

Added Genes For Natural Pesticieds

As genetically engineered crops are developed, an early use for genetic engineering may be in creating breeds that are naturally resistant to insect pests. So far the techniques for doing this have mostly been tested out in the tobacco plant, for the reasons already described. So it is important to remember that the techniques described here will become available for wheat, rice and other cereals as soon as techniques for inserting genes into cereals become reliable.

Dr. Angharad Gatehouse of Durham University – an important centre for plant genetic engineering – has discovered several different chemicals produced by various plants which naturally repel or kill insect pests without harming any other life. She looks forward to a day when all major crops will be protected by batteries of added genes for such chemicals, each gene protecting against a different pest in a different way. One of the first natural pesticides she discovered is produced by the cow pea plant. It inhibits the production of the digestive juice trypsin by the stomachs of beetles which feed on the cow pea. Without trypsin, the beetle cannot digest any protein and so starves to death in a couple of days.

Dr. Gatehouse has taken the gene for the trypsin inhibitor out of the cow pea plant into tobacco plants, and shown they are protected against insect pests, including those which also pray on cereals. So this technique will work for cereals too, when genes can be added to them.

Borrowing Bacterial Pesticides

Cow peas, and indeed green plants generally, aren't the only living things in which genes for resistance to pests are being sought. Plant Genetic Systems of Ghent in Belgium, have found the genes for a natural pesticide in a bacterium, Bacillus thuringiensis, which is so toxic to many insects that the bacterium itself is already used as a natural pesticide. But it is expensive to use. The Belgian company have taken the gene out of B. thuringiensis and put it into tobacco, using Agrobacterium. The plants with the added gene were protected against the caterpillars of the tobacco hornworm, a major pest.

By now you can see that Agrobacterium is very important in plant genetic engineering. At Durham University again, Dr. Charlie Shaw has found another way to use it to protect plants against pests. His technique is very ingenious and deserves to be described, although it does take a little explaining:

If the root of a plant is damaged, then chemicals leak out of it. These act as a stimulant to any Agrobacteria in the soil nearby. As soon as they pick up the scent from a wounded root the bacteria come wriggling through the soil towards it, following the route along which the scent gets stronger and stronger, like a pack of hounds. When the scent gets very strong then the Agrobacteria "know" it will soon be time to infect the plant, to move in through the wound which allows them access. At that point a genetic switch in the bacteria comes into play and switches on the genes whose products are needed for the complete process of infection and gene insertion.

'Anti-sense' genes carrying nonsense messages to defeat infection.

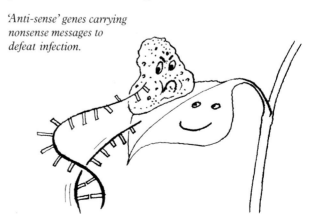

Dr Shaw has taken Agrobacteria and inserted genes into them for some of the natural pesticides which protect other bacteria against insect pests. He has linked these genes to the genetic switch which is normally linked to the genes responsible for infection. The result is that when agrobacteria genetically engineered in this way approach a wounded root by following its scent, at the point where the scent becomes strong enough to switch on the genes for infection, something else happens. Instead of moving into the plant, the engineered agrobacteria start to produce natural pesticides to protect it.

A BIOCHEMICAL BODYGUARD

The wounded plant is protected by a biochemical bodyguard of agrobacteria in a close ring around it, producing natural protective pesticides. Once the root has healed and is no longer vulnerable to insect pests (which are as keen to gain entry through wounds as are bacteria), the root will no longer leak chemicals and attract bacteria. The bacterial bodyguard's protective genes will be switched off and it will disperse.

SUBTLE ADVANTAGES

There are subtle advantages to this ingenious scheme. It gets round the problem of getting genes into monocotyledons. The protective genes are inserted into bacteria, not into plants. Even when a way of getting genes into monocotyledons is perfected, making plants produce their own pesticides rather than using bacteria will have a disadvantage. Producing pesticides will place an extra burden on a plant's resources of energy and chemicals, leaving it that much less effort to put into making the wanted food substances. Making bacteria produce the pesticide instead takes the burden off the plant.

But if soil bacteria were simply given extra genes to make them produce pesticides, then they, like the plants, would have to devote some of their resources to an activity of no value to them. Consequently, the bacteria would soon lose out in competition with other soil bacteria with no such altruistic burden enforced upon them. Dr Shaw's

technique of making the bacteria produce pesticides only when they come close to a plant which is specially vulnerable because it has been wounded leaves the bacteria with much less of a handicap. Nor is the potential for the technique limited to pesticides. Genes for enzymes which destroy soil fungi have been put into agrobacteria, and have also been shown to provide protection.

ANTI-SENSE GENES

Another ingenious technique being developed, and in at least one case already used commercially to improve crops, is the use of Anti-Sense genes. As their name implies, these artificial genes carry nonsense messages which are the precise opposites of messages carried by natural genes. The messages sent from antisense genes implanted into crop plants can be used, experiments have shown, to cancel out the messages from the genes of viruses which have infected cells and are starting to try to replicate.

A virus infects a cell with particles containing viral genes made of DNA. The virus reproduces by using the infected cell's machinery to make copies of the viral genes in the form of RNA. These are sent out to the ribosomes, the organelles in the cell where new protein molecules are made, in accordance with the instructions carried by the sequences of bases in the RNA messengers copied off the DNA genes. The ribosomes obediently make viral proteins. The process of replication, of making new virus particles in the infected cell, has begun. Normally it is then unstoppable.

But if the plant has been given an antisense gene, which is the mirror image of the gene for some vital component of the virus, then the virus can be prevented from replicating. At the same time as the virus's genes are producing their messengers, their RNA copies, the antisense gene will be producing its messenger, its RNA copy. When this encounters its opposite number of viral RNA the two messenger molecules stick together along their lengths, as two complementary opposite sequences of DNA or RNA always do. This completely prevents the virus's message getting through to the ribosome and being translated into protein. For that to happen, the RNA molecule has to be a naked single strand.

Making an anti-sense gene is quite simple. First, the gene is selected which is to be cancelled out, perhaps the gene for a vital viral enzyme. Then the gene is cloned in the labortory and two of its bells and whistles: the little sequence at the start of the gene which says "Start reading instructions here", known as the promoter, and the little sequence at the end which says "Stop reading my instructions here", known as the terminator, are identified. These are snipped off, swopped around, and re-attached. Now the gene will be read from back to front instead of from front to back.

Nature thought of the idea first. At least one bacterium is known to use anti-sense genes as a means of regulating its metabolism. Anti-sense genes should have no effects on anything except the genes they cancel out. In theory, at least, it should be possible to implant several antigenes so as to protect against several different viruses. But doing so will have to wait for that vital breakthrough in engineering monocotyledons.

Delaying Ripening

Anti-sense genes can potentially be used in other ways. ICI Seeds, working with Nottingham

Genetically engineered tomatoes....

University, are using them to control the ripening of tomatoes. Ripening is largely caused by an enzyme which breaks down cell walls and plays a key part in the process whereby the tomato changes from being hard, green and bitter to being soft, red and sweet. The antisense version of the

gene for the enzyme (polygalacturonase) has been made and inserted into tomato plants, the fruits of which then produce much less enzyme and ripen more slowly.

Will Antisense Protect Humans?

It has been suggested that anti-sense genes might one day be implanted into farm animals, and even into people, to protect them too against diseases. At present the idea of implanting any genes which would be handed on to future generations into humans is viewed with abhorrence. But as I have suggested earlier, once the implanting of anti-sense and other protective genes into animals has been shown to be effective in protecting against unpleasant diseases, and to be without side effects, then it may be that eventually there will be a rising swell of demand for it for people too.

A biotechnology which could offer you your children and forthcoming generations protection against diseases such as AIDS, for example, without any need for injections, is bound to have its attractions for many. If most scientists are asked about such possibilities, they are understandably unwilling to appear as if they might conceivably be in favour of germ line genetic engineering, and will tend to evade the question. They'll say that such techniques are far away from any conceivable human use. But far away, I suspect, means thirty or forty years.

There are other genetic engineering techniques that might eventually protect people as well as plants and animals against viruses. One such was discovered accidentally – serendipitously, as scientists like to say, by Dr. John Lomonosoff of the John Innes Research Institute near Norwich. Lomonosoff was working on tobacco mosaic virus, a virus responsible for an important disease of the tobacco plant. One gene seemed to be particularly vital for the virus to be able to replicate inside infected cells. So as to learn more about this gene, he took it out of the virus and inserted the gene on its own into tobacco plants, to see what effects it might have without the rest of the viral DNA.

In January 1991 I telephoned George

Lomonosoff about the startling result of this experiment. His response was exuberant: "I was extremely surprised when we found that if we took the plants which had been made into transgenic plants, harbouring the gene from the virus, and later inoculated these plants with the complete tobacco virus, the virus was completely incapable of replicating or of causing any illness to the plant."

Just why inserting a single gene from a virus into a plant should protect that plant against future infection with the virus the gene came from, is unknown at the time of writing. It looks at first sight as if something equivalent to vaccination has gone on, but that isn't really so. The viral protein made by the inserted gene does not stimulate anything like an immune response in the plant. But whatever the explanation, this startling discovery may have a lot of potential for protecting crops and perhaps animals too against virus diseases. Cucumbers and peas are affected by viruses very similar to tobacco mosaics, and they are likely first targets for similar protection.

Beyond that, Lomonosoff believes he may find a similar gene in many other viruses. "What we'd like to do" he explained, "is to take the equivalent gene from other plant viruses which infect other commercially important crops and insert the gene into those crops, to see if we can make them resistant to disease in the same way."

Some viruses that infect animals appear to have a similar gene, suggesting they might be protected in the same way as plants. Not only does this perhaps offer a completely new means of protection, but as Lomonosoff points out, the protection it provides is complete, not partial.

Once again one has to ask whether this technique, if it proves effective in creating virus resistant animals as well as plants, will not eventually come to be used for humans too. Will the public really stand for farm animals being better protected against disease then they are themselves?

POISON CAPSULES

A gene-swopping technique which will,

hopefully, help considerably to improve food supplies in Africa, involves sorghum, a staple food crop in the semi-arid tropics in Asia as well as Africa. A major problem in these areas is the plant disease Anthracnose, caused by a fungus infecting sorghum. Some sorghum plants have natural resistance to anthracnose, but others are highly susceptible.

Drs Ralph Nicholson and Beth Snyder of the Department of Botany in Purdue University in the USA discovered that when a fungal spore lands on a sorghum leaf and starts to grow, the plants react quickly, by the standards of plants. Only two hours later, tiny round bodies appear in the cells of the leaf nearest to the threatening fungus. The bodies move towards the fungus, changing colour to a deep red and growing as they move. When they arrive at the invading fungus the bodies burst, liberating their poisonous contents, which kill the fungus – and, inevitably, the plant cells nearest to it. But because only a few cells are killed the damage to the sorghum plant itself is negligible.

One way these findings are being put to work is to discover which gene or genes are responsible for the fungus-killing mechanisms and to implant more such genes into sorghum plants. The Purdue team are also trying to transplant the genes into cereals which have little natural resistance to fungus diseases. That could have a huge commercial impact.

SUICIDE PILLS FOR WEEDS

There is another way in which the findings could be put to work. Resistant sorghum plants are stimulated to produce their poisons, known as phytoalexins, by chemicals released from fungal spores as they begin to germinate and to grow a tube to invade a sorghum leaf. When these chemicals are released in minute quantities from a single fungal spore, their effect is to make just a few cells locally produce phytoalexins. So it is only these few cells that are killed along with the fungus when the phytoalexins are released. Tests at Purdue have shown that if the Elicitors, as these chemicals are called, are made in large quantities artificially and applied to sorghum leaves, then

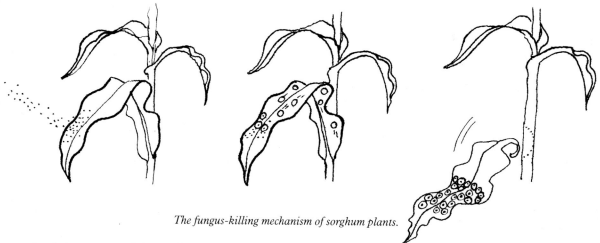

The fungus-killing mechanism of sorghum plants.

much larger quantities of phytoalexins are produced, which kill many of the leaf cells producing them. If the dose is large enough, the whole plant is killed.

An environmentally friendly herbicide might be made from elicitors, which would be used to destroy common species of weeds which are of the same plant family as sorghum. So long as no crop of sorghum was growing in the vicinity, a spray of synthetic elicitor would stimulate any sorghum-type weeds in the areas to bump themselves off, with a massive overdose of their own self-produced poison.

PROPAGATING FRUIT TREES

Plant genetic engineering is being developed for other purposes besides providing inbuilt resistance to pests and disease. It is, for example, being used to propagate apple trees more effectively. Once fruit farmers have a fruit tree that produces plenty of the right kind of fruit, then what they want is more of exactly that same kind of tree. They do not want to allow their trees to be fertilised as a means of reproducing, since that means bringing in many unwanted genes from another tree. They prefer to replicate their fruit trees vegetatively, by taking cuttings or layering stems into the soil to form roots and grow into new trees.

These are techniques familiar to gardeners as a means of producing trees which are genetic carbon copies of their parents. But unfortunately some of the most valuable varieties of trees – such as apple trees – cannot be propagated in this way, because trees will not grow from cuttings, and if their stems are buried in the ground they won't take root.

Now French scientists at the Biological Laboratory of the Institute for Agricultural Research at Versailles have found a way to propagate apple trees and other trees that can't be propagated by layering (burying their stems). This is done by using soil bacteria which have the magical property of making stems buried near them turn into roots. What happens is that the bacteria send some of their genes into the stem, and these genes direct the transformation into a root.

Dr. David Tepfer leads the team doing this work at Versailles. While at present he is using the soil bacteria themselves to induce root formation, his target is to isolate and clone the gene which the bacteria insert into stems to make them behave like roots, and to insert this gene into apple tree stems so that they will take root automatically. Meanwhile the bacteria have already been used to make roots grow in many different plants and trees, over one hundred species in all. The technique works in peach and pear as well as apple trees.

AN ANSWER TO PUBLIC CONCERN

David Tepfer sees this as a means of bypassing public suspicion of foodstuffs containing added genes. As he told me "We hope it will be a way of getting round the problem of having foreign genes in the fruits which are going to be consumed by humans or animals. Instead, we can put genes only into the stems but have their effects felt throughout the plant. We have shown that proteins produced by genes added to the stems and roots are carried to the aerial parts of the plants and remain there." So this technique could provide beneficial effects of added genes without their actual presence.

There is, after all, nothing unnatural about adding genes from a soil bacterium into a plant. Agrobacterium does it all the time. What genetic engineers are doing is to add extra genes to those that the bacteria add naturally.

MALE STERILITY: ALL-ROUND BENEFIT

Lastly in these examples of plant genetic engineering, here's something which is confidently expected to increase world rice production by 15%,

Male sterility in plants.

and to save corn growers 100 million dollars every year in the USA alone. It will also benefit farmers growing tomatoes, wheat, potatoes, cabbages and many other crops. This new technique is a new way to make the male organs of plants sterile – unable to produce pollen. Guaranteed male sterility will be an enormous benefit, to seed suppliers as well as to farmers.

Hybrid vigour is a concept familiar to anyone who has noted the difference in pets between the rather listless pedigree products of excessive inbreeding and the sparkle and vigour of mongrels and moggies derived from chance matings (with partners chosen by the animals themselves, not their owners). The scientific basis for hybrid vigour is still obscure. But hybrid crops grown from seed with two well-separated parents are much more vigorous, hardy and productive. So as to produce guaranteed hybrid seed, plants have to be prevented from fertilising themselves. This can be tricky as many crops have male and female organs on the same plant.

Today plants are made male sterile in several ways, all of them unsatisfactory and consuming vast quantities of time and labour, most commonly by removing the tiny male organs by hand. There are of course some mutant strains of cereals which are naturally male sterile, but they have become excessively inbred, which carries its own hazards. Complete corn crops have been wiped out by blight because the entire crops consisted of one male sterile, highly vulnerable strain.

THE "GENETIC LASER"

The new technique of sterilizing plants devised by Robert Goldberg of the University of California at Los Angeles and a team at Plant Genetic Systems in Ghent in Belgium, has been nicknamed the "Genetic Laser" because of its precision. Pollen is produced in male organs, anthers, and nourished as it grows by a layer of cells surrounding the growing pollen, the tapetum. Goldberg identified a gene which is activated only in the tapetum, and coupled this gene to another gene, to produce an enzyme which destroys the RNA messages sent into cells by genes when the genes are expressed. Such messages are essential for the growth of cells.

The coupling of the gene for the message-destroying enzyme to the gene that is only active in the tapetum provides the genetic laser. Plants into which the combined gene are inserted are unable to form a tapetum. With no tapetum to nourish it, they are also unable to make pollen. So they are male sterile. Because the gene is only

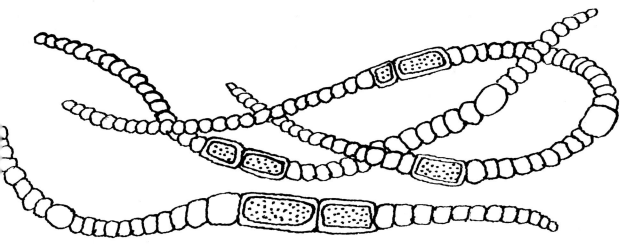

Anabena: a water-living organism. Geneticists are currently trying to transfer its nitrogen-fixing enzymes into plants.

activated in the tapetum, the rest of the plant is unaffected by this ingenious genetic engineering.

The first use of this technique is planned for oil seed rape in 1992. Once the genes can be inserted into monocotyledons routinely, Robert Goldberg and Jan Vermans of Plant Genetic Systems believe their technique will boost the yields of many of the world's major crops by anything from 10 to 40% within a few years.

PLANTS THAT FIX THEIR OWN NITROGEN

Nitrogen liberated into the atmosphere by the breakdown of plant and animal tissues in the soil is recaptured by nitrogen fixing bacteria. Some of these live in nodules on the roots of the plants known as legumes, such as peas and beans. Others are free-living, such as the filamentous blue-green algae Anabaena. One species lives in the guts of termites and supplies them with the nitrogen which they wouldn't normally get in sufficient quantities out of their staple diet of wood.

One of the first declared aims of plant genetic engineers was to try to transfer the genes for nitrogen-fixing enzymes from bacteria into plants themselves, in the hope that new strains of rice and wheat could be created which would have no need for nitrogenous fertilisers. These fertilizers are expensive to manufacture and to buy because of the large amounts of energy consumed in their making. A number of different genes have turned out to be involved. There is no technical reason why they should not be transferred from the bacteria in which they are naturally found, into plants (beyond the temporary problem of getting any genes into monocotyledons). But nitrogen-fixing bacteria live in the absence of oxygen and their nitrogen-fixing enzymes are destroyed by oxygen. So if they are to work in plants, the added genes would have to be expressed, and their enzymes made only in parts of the plant with very low oxygen concentrations.

A further problem could be that plants with built-in nitrogen fixing genes might use up so much energy fixing nitrogen that they became undersized and uneconomical to grow. All in all, crops that fix their own nitrogen probably require a third generation of super-sophisticated genetic engineering manoeuvres. Maybe early in the next century.

SUPERWEEDS?

I hope these few examples make it clear that many crops will soon benefit from genetic engineering and that the benefits will be widespread. A question that is rightly asked is, whether the release of plants with added genes into the environment may do harm in the long term. Certainly in some – not most – areas there is need for care and precautions. For example, there is a clear need for the most extreme precautions to prevent genes for resistance to herbicides engineered into crop plants becoming transferred into weeds of the same species as the crop plant, by cross-fertilisation. But resistance to herbicides is a special case. There is also a mistaken idea around that adding genes to crop plants for the sorts of purposes described here may somehow transform a crop into a super-weed. But scientists agree that this won't happen. The success of 'superweeds' is, invariably, the consequence of numerous genes working together in a collaboration which has evolved over long periods. We are not going to create that kind of co-ordinated efficiency by injecting one or two genes for specific characteristics designed to benefit the consumer, not the crop plant.

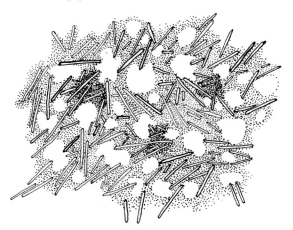

The tobacco mosaic virus.

In the early days of genetic engineering experiments, those who drew up careful safety guidelines for experiments argued that genes inserted artificially into living things might behave differently from genes moving around naturally. There was no reason why they should, but we couldn't be sure. Now 18 years experience (the first gene was moved from one organism to another in 1973) has shown that genes don't have strange, unpredictable effects when they are moved artificially from one organism to another. They just do what they did before, only much less efficiently until they are made to feel at home by tacking on extra bells and whistles.

WHO OWNS RAINFOREST GENES?

Concern is felt over the exploitation of plant genes originating in the developing, tropical world for purposes which may most benefit the rich, industrialised world. The developing world is more dependent upon trade in biological products, which biotechnology can, potentially, either improve, or replace with products made in the developed world. There is now the beginning of awareness (brought about largely by Professor Alan Bull at Kent University) that genetic resources in microorganisms are as worthy of conservation as are vanishing species of macroorganisms. They may even be of far greater use to the world. More genes for enzymes which will work at high temperatures and break down complex chemical pollutants, as well as genes for natural substances with pharmaceutical potential, are waiting to be found in the rain forests. Who do these genes belong to?

Scientists at the independent Panos Institute work to promote sustainable development in Third World countries. They have identified that the real challenge to developing countries, to aid donors, and to big multinational pharmaceutical and chemical companies is to ensure that biotechnology is applied with a just return for any Southern genes (genes from the developing world) that are used. The developing world is also concerned that its resources may be exploited for purposes which will not be beneficial – and perhaps even harmful. But developing nations are not opposed to biotechnology in itself. African and Asian scientists are too aware of its potential to help solve their problems for that. If the West were to turn its back on genetic engineering, it would continue to be exploited eagerly in the tropics.

CHAPTER 13

ABRAHAM LINCOLN AND THE FIRST AMERICANS

DNA is a tough molecule, with an ability to survive for very long periods in unfavourable conditions. This is now allowing scientists to clone genes from long-dead people and animals. Very recently some startlingly long strides have been taken back into the past in this way.

In July 1990, British Museum officials gave the go-ahead to Dutch scientists to test for the presence of the AIDS virus in mummified Egyptians and their pet monkeys dating back to 3,500BC. The tests are testing the theory that the virus was present in a harmless form for thousands of years before recently mutating and becoming deadly.

MUTATED HIV?

Dr Jaap Goudsmit of the Amsterdam Medical Centre and Dr Rutger Perizonius of Utrecht university plan to use the Polymerase Chain Reaction (PCR) described in chapter 2. They are searching for a virus which they believe may have been present in a harmless, "passenger" form. The technique is exactly the same as that which was used in the UK to demonstrate that a British sailor had died with AIDS in 1959, though the condition was not recognised in Britain until 23 years later.

Another theory of the origin of the AIDS epidemic is that the virus originated in monkeys and spread to man. Hence the search for virus in

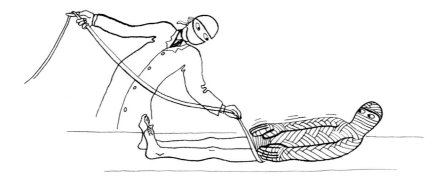

New life for mummies?

the mummified monkeys. The tests will not harm either human or monkey mummies, as only tiny pieces of tissue one centimetre across are needed.

LINCOLN: AN HEREDITARY AILMENT?

Rather a different kind of question will, it is hoped, be answered by analysing DNA from blood shed by President Abraham Lincoln during his assassination, on April 14th 1865, by John Wilkes Booth in a Washington theatre. The US National Museum of Health and Medicine in Washington has samples of blood stains from the cuffs of a doctor who attended Lincoln, and locks of hair and bone fragments which, between them, must contain more than enough DNA to answer some interesting questions. Why was Lincoln so tall and thin? Why did he suffer from chronic depression? The answer could be that he was affected by Marfan syndrome, an hereditary ailment which makes those affected develop abnormally long and weak bones. They often also have weak eyes and weak hearts, and are frequently affected by chronic depression.

Is it right to submit dead people to such tests? Marc Micozzi is the Director of the US National Museum and he took pains to make clear how carefully the project would be handled: "Before we make any decisions as to how tests should be done, we need to consider the ethical implications. We will be calling together a panel of experts to recommend whether or not to proceed with the tests. The first issue is the rights of a dead person to medical privacy. On Lincoln's death the comment was 'Now he belongs to the ages'. But we're not sure whether that applies to his DNA."

The debate as to whether Lincoln was affected by Marfan syndrome has been going on for thirty years. The museum doctors who hope to make the tests argue that people affected by the same condition today would be greatly heartened to know that such a great man shared and overcame their affliction.

DNA can be preserved for much longer than that being taken from Egyptian mummies. Genes taken from corpses interred 7,500 years ago are being studied in the USA, in an attempt to answer questions about the first inhabitants of the Americas and their resistance to disease.

GENES FROM A PREHISTORIC BURIAL GROUND

The terrible effects of some European illnesses upon the native populations of the Americas are well documented. But just why American Indians have such generally poor resistance to imported bacteria and viruses is less well understood. Near the East coast of Florida is a peat bog waterlogged with acid water which has preserved the remains of 165 people in what is thought to have been a peaceful prehistoric burial ground. They may provide the answer. Unlike corpses in similar bogs in the UK, there are no signs of injury in the corpses in the Windover pond, as it's called, in Florida. Parts of them – the cranium, some brain tissue, the skeleton and some body tissues – are well preserved – and so are their genes.

The 165 people in the Windover pond were interred between 6,990 and 8,130 years ago, (as established by radiocarbon dating). This means that only a very few generations had elapsed after their ancestors had arrived in Florida as part of one of the first of several successive waves of immigrants who moved across a land bridge from Asia, where the Behring straits are now, and down through Central America into Latin America.

Professor Peter Parham and his colleagues in Stanford University in California and Florida University have made DNA probes designed to pick out a particular type of gene, the so-called HLA genes which are largely responsible for the control of the immune system. He used the probes to pick out the HLA genes from samples of tissue from all the bodies in the Windover pond. Then PCR was used to copy the genes millions of times over.

Professor Parham told me that "HLA genes were chosen because they are genes that show tremendous variation between populations of humans in different places and in different ethnic groups. It is probable that in different parts of the world where there are different diseases, particular forms of these molecules and the genes responsible for them have been selected. One interesting question is going to be whether the types of genes that we see in this population will be similar to the ones we see today, and in particular whether they reflect the types of genes that one finds in the modern-day American Indian population."

WHY AMERICAN INDIAN IMMUNITY IS LIMITED

Professor Parham points out that the American Indian populations of today are quite strikingly lacking in diversity of HLA genes compared to populations in Europe. The greater the diversity of HLA genes in a population, the greater the chances of some members of a population having the genes needed to resist a virus or bacterium new to that population.

One explanation of the lack of diversity could be a 'Founder' effect. That is, the reason for small numbers of HLA genes may be because only small numbers of brave people took part in the hazardous invasion of the Americas across the Behring straits and down through unknown terrority.

Another explanation could be that the American Indians have suffered so many imported epidemics over the last few hundred years that the numbers of HLA genes originally present have been reduced to those few which give their owners some resistance to European diseases – all the rest have been wiped out. If the HLA genes from the Windover pond are few in number, like those of American Indians today, that will support the first hypothesis. If they are more numerous, then it is likely that epidemics wiping out whole populations have been the origin of such a small remaining diversity in HLA genes.

The analysis of ancient genes has taken huge leaps in just a couple of years, and Professor Parham believes it will remain a growth area. He has shown that specific types of genes such as HLA genes can be selected, picked out and analysed using the magic of PCR. Museums with huge collections of preserved specimens will use tiny samples of tissue to explore the relationships of extinct species more precisely. The analysis of DNA from living species has already provided surprises about their evolutionary relationships. Exploring DNA from ancient, even extinct species will add yet another dimension to such research.

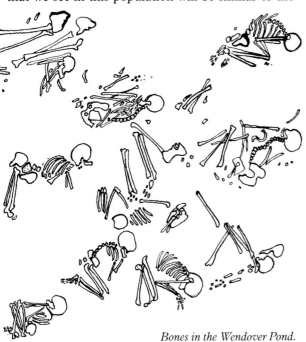

Bones in the Wendover Pond.

CHAPTER 14

POSTSCRIPT

And lastly – the Biocomputer. We have already seen that biotechnology and genetic engineering will increasingly dominate the making of drugs and vaccines in the next millennium, and make greater inroads into chemical industry, via biotransformations by enzymes and catalytic antibodies. Now the field of micro-electronics is also being invaded. Computers made, if not out of flesh then at least out of blood cells, may be on the way.

A startling series of experiments are currently being conducted by Professor Sligar at the University of Illinois in the USA. He is experimenting with proteins, including haemoglobin – the red oxygen-carrying pigment in the blood – and cytochromes, the enzymes which break down food with oxygen to release energy to power living cells. Some such proteins, including chlorophyll, can absorb light and turn its energy into electric current. Some of them set up currents as part of the chemical reactions they catalyse.

These properties are what are wanted by people designing microelectronic circuitry – and more recently optical circuitry in which signals are carried by light beams instead of electric currents. Of course protein molecules don't manipulate light and electricity in exactly the ways required by circuit designers and computer builders. But by cloning the genes for the proteins, and altering the genes, the electrical properties of the proteins can be altered. This kind of protein engineering is just getting underway.

In this way, Professor Sligar has already altered the electrical and optical properties of his proteins. He has improved their ability to pass signals to each other, and equipped them with molecular hooks so that the proteins can attach themselves to surfaces in ordered rows. The next stage – just getting underway – is to pass tiny currents through these orderly rows of protein proto-chips, and to see how the currents are modulated.

The electrical products of the future… grown from proteins.

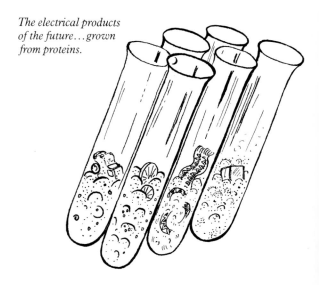

It begins to sound like real live circuitry – and with advantages to make the highly competitive electronics industry prick up its ears. Proteins used as chips would be thousands of time smaller than their silicon equivalents, so they would work much faster. They would also conduct electricity without heating up. That solves another problem which plagues computer designers: how to get rid of the heat which ever-more compact devices generate. Ordered arrays of proteins lend themselves naturally to assembly into parallel processors – advanced computers which carry out many different processes simultaneously, mimicking the human brain. Once we know how to change the genes to get the required results, it won't be expensive to grow protein chips in bioreactors.

Professor Sligar is convinced that the interface between genetic engineering, electro-optics and semiconductor science will be an explosive growth area. It is an interface which is literal as well as metaphorical. Already, German scientists have succeeded in linking a living nerve cell (from a leech) to a piece of silicon, and have measured the electric currents which were produced by the nerve cell and picked up by the silicon. It will soon be easy to link biocomputers and other devices such as biosensors (a device in which an antibody or enzyme is used to detect minute quantities of the chemical it reacts with) to more orthodox circuitry.

The boundary between life and non-life is becoming blurred. It may be that in less than a hundred years, the distinction will have gone altogether. Maybe we will grow our household appliances as well as our computers; our fridges and carpets and washing machines, even our houses and cars may be living organisms. How much of our technology will be biotechnology in, say, two hundred years! Maybe most. Maybe nearly all. We are only at the beginning of an unimagineable journey, far stranger than science fiction. But you and I and our children can chart its course. We can control what we create.

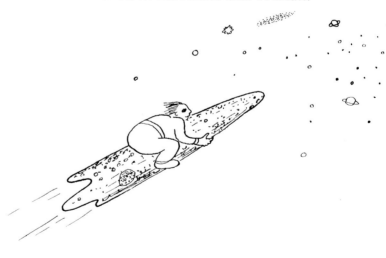

INDEX

Please note: Since the book is primarily about genetic engineering, many terms for example genetic engineering, genes, biotechnology are used frequently. They are used in the index only when some relevant information is given.

aborted foetuses 16
abortion avoidance 34,36
abortion ethics 16,34, 38-40
abzymes 55, 79-80, 82
ADA genetic defect 23
adenine 17,19
aflatoxin 70
aging postponed 43
Agricultural Research Institute, versailles 99
agriculture 54-5,85
        and genetic engineering 93 see also enzymes
Agrobacterium tumefaciens 93-6
AIDS 23
        tests on Egyptian mummies 103
        treatment 42
        vaccines 24,58-9,62
Almond, Professor Jeffrey 58
Alzheimer's desease 16
American Indian's disease resistance 104-5
Amgen (California) 88
amino acids 14 17
Amsterdam mediacl Centre 103
anaemia treatments 43
Anderson, Dr. French 23
animal use ethics 84-5
anthracnose 98
antibodies 14,48-55
        B-cells 49, 57
        in cancer treatments 50,52,55
        as a cash crop 54
        definitions 49,54,80
        as enzymes/abenzymes 80-1
        hybridomas 49,53
        lymophocytes 48-9
        mass-produced 53
        monoclonal 49-50
        and plant diseases 55
        and pollution 55
        storage 53
        T-cells 48-9,57
antigens 50-1
anti-sense genes 96-8
antitrypsin 86
Archaeus technology 79
armadilloes 62-3
arterial endothelial cells 29

arteries, repair of 29
artificial hearts and blood vessels 29-30
atherosclerosis 30
auto-immune diseases 46-7 52
AZT 59

Babraham Institute of Animal Physiology and Genetic Research 86-7
bacillus stearothermophilus 77
Bacillus thuringiensis 95
bacteria 76-9,93-6
        in enzyme manufacture 76-7
        thermophylic 21
bacteriophages, antibodies stored in 53
bases (genetic codes) 17,20
Basle University 43
'bells and whistles' 18,21
bilharzia 61-2
Biocomputer 106-7
Bioethics Conference 1988 38
bioreactors 16
biosensors 82,107
biotechnology 10-11,16
blood cell diseases 23,28,29,46 see also AIDS, haemophilia, leukaemia
blood clots/clotting 30,82,83,86 see also haemophilia
blood substitute 46
Bodmer, Professor Sir walter 71
Boehringer Pharmaceuticals 44
bone marrow 49
Bovine Growth Hormone 86
Brenner, Professor Sydney 73
Brownlees, Professor George 28
Buchan, Dr. Alex 79
Buck, Professor Ken 94
Bull, Professor Alan 78,102
Burns, Dr. Richard 76,78

Calgene (California) 94
California University
        Berkeley 74
        Cell Microbiology Dept 78
Cambridge Laboratory for Molecular Biology 11,49,52,73
Cancer
        breast 69
        causes 68
        cervical 66
        liver 70
        lung 69
        treatments 42,50,52,67
Cancer Research Centre, Heidelberg 52
Cantor, Professor Charles 74
Capron, Professor Andrew 62

cardiovascular disease 23
cecropins 91
cellulose digestion 86-7
Cetus Corporation 20
chemical industry 37,55,85
        enzyme use in 75-6
chirality 75
chromosomes 17
Clark, Dr. John 86
cloning 19
Columbia National University 59
Colony Stimulating Factors 42
Columbia University (New York) 62
common cold 44-5
Council for International Organisation of Mediacl Sciences 39
Crampton, Dr. Julian 89-90
Crick, Francis 13,17,72
crops
        disease resistant 13
        genetic engineering with 94-5,100
        male sterility 100
Crystal, Dr. Ronald 34
cystic fibrosis 23,27,31,33-4
cytochromes 106
cytokines 18
cytosine 17,19

dairy products 86
David the Bubble Boy 23
defective genes 15
        ADA 23
        Hunter's Syndrome 34
        muscular dystrophy 37,31,32
        neurofibromatosis 34
        retinoblastoma 69
        severe immune deficiency 24
        sickle cell anaemia 23,31
        spinal muscular atrophies 34
deoxyribonucleic acid see DNA
diabetes 23,27,29, 47

DNA
        Introns 73
        long lasting 104
        polymorphisms 21,32
        pseudogenes 71-2
        replication 19-20
        spacers 71
        structure 17,19-20,74
        see also genes

DNA Polymerase 20
DNA probe 31
Dulwich Hospital 51
Durham University 94,95

dwarfism 28,43
Dystrophin 32,50

Edinburgh Institute of Animal
Physiology 88
EF 1-Alpha protein 43
Egyptian mummies 103
emphysema 86
energy saving 76
enzymes 14,20,55
   definition 80-1
   in agriculture 83-8
   in industry 55,75-9
   see also abzymes,
specific enzymes
erythropoietin 42-3

Factor IX 86
familial hypercholesterolaemia 27
farm animals
   disease resistant 14
   gene therapy 37
   transgenic 86-7
fibroblast growth factor 43
Florida University 105
Focht, Professor Dennis 78
foetal testing see defective gene
food industry 71,79,88
food substitutes 79
forensic evidence 19
Friedman, Professor Theodore 11
fruit flies 43

Gatehouse, Dr. Angharad 95
Gehring, Dr. Walter 43
geminiviruses 94
gene 'squirting' 32-3
gene therapy 13,18,22
   germ line 36-7, 38-40
   heart disease 27,30
   safety 25, 45-6
   skin grafts 28
   somatic 36,38
   viruses in 23-4
'Gene Theraputics' 33
genes
   animal expressed in plants 54
   anti-sense 96-8
   cancer 68-70
   cloning 18,19
   definition 14,17
   expressed 15
   heredity 14-17
   HLA 105
   inserting into bacteria 82
   inserting into cells 13, 23-4
   marker 29
   protective 27
   pseudogenes 71-2
   Rb 69-70
   suppressed 15

'switches' 15-16
tumour suppressor 69,70
viral 24
genetic code 17-18,53
genetic defects 15,23
   diagnosis 21,25,32
   see also defective genes, DNA, gene
therapy
genetic engineering
   bad image 10,85
   in cellulose digestion 86-7
   definition 13-14
   ethics 11,38-40,86-8
   germ line 38-40,97
   hazards 45-6
   and herbicide resistance 93
   public awareness 11,37,86
   regulations 11
   in tree propagation 99
   and tropical diseases 56,89
   uses and misuses 9
Genetic Laser 100
germ line engineering 97
germ line therapy 37,38-40
Glasgow University 66
Goldberg, Dr. Robert 100-1
Goudsmit, Dr Jaap 103
Green, Professor Howard 28
growth factors 43
growth hormones 18,28,33
guanine 17,19

haemoglobin 106
haemophilia B 28,83
Halling, Dr. Peter 91
Ham, Dr. Peter 91
Hammersmith Hospital 35
'Handbook of Man' 71
Hardman, Dr. David 76,77
Harvard Medical School 28,32
Haslow, Dr. David 61
Hepatitis B 61,70
hepatocytes 27
herbicide resistance 93,102
heredity and defective genes 14
herpes 61
Hiatt, Dr. Andrew 54,82
HIV 24,45,58-9
Hoffman, Dr. Eric 32
Hoffman, Dr. Stephen 61
Holding, Dr. Cathy 35
Human Genome Organisation (HUGO)
73
Human Genome project 71-4
human immune system 41-2,45,48,89
   see also antibodies
Hume, Cardinal Basil 35
Hunter's syndrome 34
hybridoma 49-50

ICI Seeds 94,96

Illinois University 106
Imperial Cencer Fund 71
Imperial College, London 94
influenza 61
insulin 18
interferon 18,42
interleukins 18,42,62,83
Introns 73
Ivermectin 66

Jarrett, Professor Bill 66,67
Jeffreys, Professor Alec 21
Jenner, Dr. Edward 61
John Innes Research Institute 97

Kent University 76,78,102
Kingsman, Drs. Sue and Alan 58
Kunkel, Dr. Lewis

lectins 90,91
Leicester University 21
leishmaniasos 61,62
leprosy 61,62
Lerner, Professor Richard 53
life/non-life boundary 107
Lille University 64
Lincoln, President Abraham 104
liver defects 27
Liverpool School of Tropical Medicine
89,91
Lomonosoff, Dr. John 97-8
lymphokines 42
lymphokine-activated killer cells 42

malaria 56
   mosquito control 89-90
   parasite 57,59
   vaccines 59-60
male sterility (crops) 100
Mammalian Development Research
Unit (UK) 35
Marfan syndrome 104
Marion Merrell Dow 66
Markin, Dr. Stephen 44-5
Max Planck Institute 94
melanoma 22,24
Merck, Sharpe and Dohme 66
Michigan University 29
Micozzi, Marc 104
microelectric circuitry 106
Milstein, Dr. Caesar 49,81
MIT 27
mitochondria 14
molecular archaeology 21
molecular biology 11
molecular genetics 44
Monk, Dr. Marilyn 35,36
monoclonal antibodies 49
monocotyledons 93,94
Monsanto 94
mosquitoes 89

Mulligan, Professor Richard 27,28,29
Mullis, Dr. Kary 20
multiple sclerosis 47,52
mutations 26,69

Nabel, Dr. Elizabeth 29
National Institute for Medical research (UK) 62
nerve growth factors 52
nerve growth inhibitors 52
neurofibromatosis 34
New Plant Genetics, The 92
New York University 59
Nicholson, Dr. Ralph 98
nitrogen fixation 101
Nottingham University 97
Nussenweig Drs. Ruth and Victor 59,60

Office of Human Genome Research 73
oil-eating bugs 79
onchocerciasis 66,91
oncogenes 24,68-70
optical circuitry 106
Ornidyl 66
orsomatrophin 86
Oxford University 28,58

Panos Institute 102
Papilloma virus 66-7
parasitic diseases 62-4, 89-91
Parham, Professor Peter 105
Parkinson's Disease 16
Patarryo, Dr. manuel 59
Pauling, Dr. Linus 81
Perizonius, Dr. Rutger 103
pesticides, natural and bacterial 95
phytoalexins 98
plant breeding 92
Plant genetic Systems 95,100,101
polar body 15,35-6
pollution 55,75,78,93
polychlorinated biphenyls (PCB's) 78
Polymerase Chain Reaction (PRC) 19,20
polymorphisms see DNA
pre-embryos 34-5
primer (in PCR) 21
protein molecules 14,17-18,34
protoplasts 54
pseudogenes 71-2
psychrophile bacteria 76
Purdue University 98

Reading University 58
reduction division 15,35
rejuvenation hormone 43-4
replication 19-20
reproductive cells 15
retinoblastoma 69
retroviruses 24
rheumatoid arthritis 42,47

ribonucleic acid see DNA
ribosome 20
ricin 50
ripening delay 97
river blindness 66,91
RNA 20
Rosenberg, Dr. Stephen 42

Sadoff, Dr. Gerald 60
St. Thomas's Hospital 43
salmonellae, in vaccine preparation 60-1
scar tissue 82
schistosomiasis 56,61,63-4
Schnell, Dr. Lisa 52
Schwab, Dr. Martin 52
Scripps Institute, California 53,54,82
Severe Combined Immune Deficiency 22-3,24
sex change 38
Shaw, Dr. Charlie 95-6
Sheppard, Dr. John 43
skin grafts 28
Sligar, Professor 106-7
smallpox vaccine 61
smoking and genes 70
Snyder, Dr. Beth 98
somatic gene therapy 38,40
Somatogen (California) 46
Sorghum 98-9
spinal muscular atrophies 43
spinal nerves 52
Stanford University 105
Stettler, Dr. Gary 46
Strathclyde University 79
strokes 30

Tepfer, Dr. David 99
'test-tube' babies 34-5
Teweles, William 92
thalassaemia 36
thalidomide 75
thymine 17,19
thermophile bacteria 76-7
thermophylic enzyme 21
thymus-dervied lymphocytes 48-9
tobacco hornworm 95
tobacco mosaic virus 97-8
transgenic animals 83-91
transgenic plants 93, 92-102
transplant organ rejection 50-1
tropical disease vaccines 56
tropical rain forests 78,102
typhoid oral vaccine 60

US National Heart, Lung and Blood Institute 34
US National Institute of Health 22,23,42,52,61,72
US National Museum of Health and Medicine 104
Utrecht University 103

vaccinia 61-2
vaccines 56-67
      multivalent 58,61-2
van der Ploeg, Professor Rex 62
Vermans, Dr. Jan 101
viruses in gene therapy 23-4, 94

Waldman, Professor Herman 51
Walter Reed Army Institute of Research 60
Walters, Leroy 38-9
Watson, James 13,17,72
Windover Pond (US) 104-5
Winter, Dr. Greg 11,53
Wisconsin University 32
Wolff, Dr. John 32-3
World Health Organisation (WHO) 66